DAILY DOSE
with Diana

Diana Scothorn

PRAISE FOR DAILY DOSE

"As a single parent running a business, I try to find balance daily: God, family and work. *Daily Dose with Diana* gives me hope and encouragement to start my day off right. In a world full of uncertainty and fear, Diana shines her light and offers wisdom and insight."
> – **Gigi Butler**, Founder of Gigi's Cupcakes and author of the *Secret Ingredient*

"All of us need encouragement. Wherever you find yourself on this journey of life, at some point along the way, encouragement will be needed. In Diana Scothorn's new book, *Daily Dose with Diana*, you and I are given the opportunity to come face-to-face with genuine encouragement from a lady who speaks from a place of personal experience. From the deepest valley to the highest mountain, and to all points in between, Diana is a living testimony of the power of Word-based encouragement – she encourages us from a place of genuine understanding. Do yourself a favor, read this book and embrace the truth contained within it; I'm quite sure you'll be glad you did. God bless you!"
> – **Dean Sikes**, Founder of THE *YOU MATTER* FOUNDATION

"I would highly recommend and endorse Diana Scothorn's new book entitled *Daily Dose with Diana*. Although I have only known her for a few years I have found her daily blogs on Facebook amazing! I love that as a prominent businesswoman in Dallas she still has time to talk to and help any man or woman on the streets. She loves and welcomes anyone and everyone that needs help. I don't believe that anyone could be a so-called "stranger" to her. Diana's words are always to the point, kind, compassionate, and so true about how life is. I find them very inspirational, scriptural, and good old common-sense facts about daily life. The book is awesome!"
> – **Sam Pollinzi**, Restored Hope Ministries

"Diana is a natural born writer and her ability to pull out spiritual truths from practical situations is also a gift. Her discipline, hard work, insight, success and commitment to excellence is an inspiration for us all!"

      – **Nicole C.**, Recording artist, Songwriter, Author

"This devotion will change your life. Whether you desire to be a success in business or to be an accomplished student, Diana's daily inspirations will give you guidance and direction. The unique thing about her book is the fact that it reaches all ages and all backgrounds. Diana's genuineness and her wealth of knowledge and experience will catapult you into your destiny and God-given purpose."

      – **Debra George**, Debra George Ministries

ACKNOWLEDGMENTS

I want to thank Sandra Gober for planting a seed to write a devotion when the thought never crossed my mind and for encouraging me continually by reading my devotionals daily.

I want to thank my dear friend Terri Savelle Foy for inspiring me to *dream big* as I believe God to do the impossible! She is a mentor and precious friend for over 20 years. It's the encouragement of others that waters the seeds that often lay dormant in our hearts.

I want to thank my husband for encouraging me to be all God created me to be. On many occasions, I thought of talking myself out of doing a devotional. I told him that there're hundreds of thousands of devotional books out there. He lovingly replied, "Baby, it does not matter how many there are. It matters that you obey God with the one He instructed you to write." He has never quit believing in me!

Thank you to my beautiful daughter and son-in-law for blessing me with eight beautiful grandchildren. They've been a great inspiration for me to share our legacy.

I want to thank my son for believing in me and the call of God on my life. His love for me and the desire I have for him to finish his race strong has inspired me to finish my race with passion.

TABLE OF CONTENTS

PREFACE

My life has been a journey filled with steps and missteps. I can remember when it felt like the wheels to my future were in reverse. For every step I appeared to be going forward, I found myself taking two steps backward. We've all been there, I'm sure, but it's how we get from where we are to where God wants us to be that is the most important lesson we can achieve. Everyone has a story, but not everyone *shares* their story. My account was hidden deep in my heart, but by God's grace I'm sharing mine.

Being raised Catholic, I had minimal vision for my life. I had no understanding of the Bible and found myself in situations where I didn't know how I got there, nor how I would be able to escape. As a child, I was sexually abused, yet my parents never knew. It was a guarded secret that stayed buried in my heart and kept me confined in my past for years.

With an ordinary American family and both parents, I was born in Tokyo and lived overseas for a total of six years before returning to the U.S. Moving from state to state, our family finally settled. I was raised in the small town of Weatherford, Texas from the time I was in fifth grade. My father served in Vietnam and returned when I was a small child. He soon emerged in his pain and memories of war, which prevented him from participating in any area of my life. He was hiding behind the pain of Vietnam, which allowed his heart to become hardened. He was unable to demonstrate love or show affection.

In desperation for the love of a father, I found myself in relationships that were below the standards of my convictions, which surrounded me in an environment that exposed me to things I should've never been exposed to. I became involved in things I would never dream a young girl from a small town would find herself. However, I managed to graduate at the top of my class with music scholarships available. Instead, I pursued my passion for fashion and modeling.

Not long afterward, I became pregnant. Suddenly, life began to swirl in a downward spiral. I was abandoned with a small child and desperately needed to be loved. I found myself compromising my standards and became pregnant in an abusive relationship that I was trapped in for years. I saw no way out.

In my desperation for more, I discovered a relationship with Jesus. It was intimate and personal. I learned His "playbook" of what to do and what not to do. As many of you know, the Bible is *the* ultimate guide for a healthy, fulfilling life. Most importantly, what I did or didn't do never changes Jesus' love for me.

Later, I found love once again, marrying a pastor's son. It seemed all my dreams had come true. After 10 years of marriage, once again I was shocked to find out that my husband had been living a double life and betrayed me. I was once again abandoned, with little hope for a future and two kids to provide for and raise on my own. It was a lonely painful season, but God is everlasting.

Waiting on God and His timing has been something I've had to work on diligently. I tend to be a driven, goal-oriented, check-it-off-my-list person. I got myself into more trouble by running ahead of God's timing. It's hard to hear that still, small whisper when you're constantly running ahead of God with His voice behind you.

Through these seasons, I've learned that our greatest strengths can also be our greatest weaknesses. My strengths are the ability to never give up and keep pressing forward. Galatians 6:9 says, "Be not weary in well doing, for in due time you will reap the harvest if you faint not." This has been my life motto. There seems to be a direct correlation between running from myself and freedom from myself. Through Jesus, I've found freedom from sin, freedom from myself and the freedom to live worthy of the call Jesus has placed on my life.

The minute I took my focus off myself and my past and placed Jesus in my present and future, I began to take giant strides into my destiny.

Over the years, I've been so grateful that I've stayed in the fight. Actually, I'm grateful that God fought for me and never gave up. When I focus on dead things, they will not change the past. However, when I focus on all God has done for me, I see a victorious life prepared ahead.

Clearly, God has protected me by not giving into my childish temper tantrums. Thinking about all the times He has spared my life, I realize all the times He gave me grace when I deserved judgment, He opened doors that the devil had shut and shut the doors the devil tried to open. When I felt unloved, He comforted me with His love. When problems arise, instead of reaching back into my old habits of worrying, I look up and reach for Jesus, knowing He holds my future.

As a result, I've gone from being a single parent desperate for hope and throwing a newspaper route to a successful business owner of a marketplace ministry. In addition, I'm an ordained minister, international speaker, wife, mother and grandmother of eight. I'm living proof that when God is *for* you nothing can come against you regardless of your upbringing, education or past. God will do exceedingly abundantly above anything you could ask, think or imagine.

I've learned walking out of our destiny is a process. The first step is a step of obedience. The second step is to trust God with every step after that. The devil wants us to quit in the middle — halfway through our destination. God sees us through until the end. I cherish the lyrics to a song that Mandisa, a Christian artist, sings, "When the devil knocks you down, stay in until the final round because you are an overcomer."

As you read each day, I pray you're encouraged and come to the revelation that you're predestined for a great life. No matter what the fight may appear to be, if you do not quit, with Jesus you are destined to win.

Release and Receive

"A time to search and a time to give up,
a time to keep and a time to throw away."
— Ecclesiastes 3:6

> *I have learned that God wants to take us from complexity to simplicity to free our lives from stress.*

The Bible says that there are good things in life that can still not be profitable for our lives. This means there are things in life that aren't necessarily bad for us to have, but aren't profitable for our future. If we rush through life striving, we can take for granted the beauty and simplicity in the things God has given us.

Over the years, I've learned that God wants to take us *from complexity* to *simplicity* to free our lives from stress. The enemy (the devil) will use stress as a way to keep us from hearing God's still, small voice, which ultimately steals our peace. As Psalm 46:10 says, "Be still and know that I am God." However, I like to paraphrase it this way — *peace is the glue that holds emotions intact.*

Peace keeps us from falling apart under pressure. When we have the peace of God, the worlds' stress can't contain the plans God has for our future. God often asks us to *release to receive.*

In my early years of my career, I managed all-women's health clubs. God clearly released me from that industry; yet, I still wanted to hang on to teaching private classes on the side. My new career required me to travel 100 miles away from home, yet I would stress my schedule to make it back several times a week to teach these classes, despite God releasing me from the industry.

I was doing a good thing and saw nothing wrong with it. I was able to help people get into good physical condition while remaining in shape myself. It was profitable for their body and my life. I wasn't doing anything harmful. Although God had instructed me otherwise, I found myself trying to reason with what *I* wanted to do. I was holding on to something God had asked me to release.

He never said I couldn't work out and stay in shape. He merely wanted to release me from the obligation and commitment, which was keeping me in a frantic state and would ultimately cause me to lose focus on my current responsibilities.

As a result, I've learned it's wise to obey God. On the other side of my prompt, obedience is a blessing for my life. There comes a necessary time to release and depart to receive in full.

LIFE LESSON: When we hang on to what we've been told to release, we can't receive what God has prepared for us to grow in.

MY PRAYER: Lord, help me let go of the things I know are cluttering my schedule and causing me undo stress. You know the things that are profitable for my life. Please help me to not only hear You, but obey. Amen.

HIS PROMISE:
"*All things are lawful [that is, morally legitimate, permissible], but not all things are beneficial or advantageous. All items are lawful, but not all things are constructive [to character] and edifying to spiritual life.*"
— 1 Corinthians 10:23

"*And we know that in all things God works for the good of those who love him, who have been called according to his purpose.*" — Romans 8:28

It's Never Too Late

"I am confident that God, who began the good work within you, will continue his work until it is finally finished on the day when Christ Jesus returns."
— Philippians 1:6

> *It's not age that determines our destiny, but the steps we take that are necessary to get there.*

It's never too late to begin. When we get the revelation that with God it's never too late is when we'll not hesitate to begin. The only thing it takes to start again is a step. It's not age that determines our destiny, but the steps we take that are necessary to get there. After a devastating divorce, I was convinced it was too late to start over. I didn't have the energy or strength to begin again.

As a result, the devil taunted me with — You will never have a forever love. You will never be able to say you're the only one. You will never find another who will love your children. It's too late, so why begin?

Even though the devil is committed to his lies, God is committed to His truth. The truth is that what God began in us in the beginning, He will see to it that it's a finished work in the end. Not by our strength, but by God's Spirit leading us. God has a future for us and it's good. He'll never leave us or forsake us. God doesn't see our age; He sees our hearts. He makes all things beautiful. If we have the heart to begin again, He'll give us the heart to finish.

God will lead you to where He's committed to taking you. When we say to the Lord that we'll take the first step, He'll walk with us the rest of the way. Too often we're wary of the end before we even begin. God never asked us to finish. He only asked us to trust Him as we begin. The devil will whisper that you must do, but Jesus says, 'It is done.' Our responsibility is to trust God in the beginning and let Him lead us to the end. It's never too late to begin.

LIFE LESSON: Nothing can set us back from the direction God intended us to go, if we trust Him with our life. When the devil tells us we are at the end, God will give us the grace to step without hesitation, to begin to live again.

MY PRAYER: Thank You Lord, that it is never too late with You. In Your time, everything is brought to completion. Give me strength to step out and begin. Your power is made perfect when I am weak. Help me to trust you to lead the way, so I will not be afraid to begin again. Amen.

HIS PROMISE:
"See, I am doing a new thing! Now it springs up; do you not perceive it? I am making a way in the wilderness and streams in the wasteland."
— Isaiah 43:19

"My grace is sufficient for you, for my power is made perfect in weakness."
— 2 Corinthians 12:9

From Victim to Victory

"I can do all things through Christ which strengtheneth me."
— Philippians 4:13 KJV

> *We don't have to remain injured. There's healing with Jesus. We can be whole.*

In my life, I've had problems that have caused hardships. The things that have happened to me weren't all my fault. I've learned we can blame our circumstances on people or we can accept that our past has *no* authority to define who we are.

What has happened to us doesn't have to reflect who we become. We have to decide to keep running toward our God-given destiny and refuse to look back. Just because someone hurt us in our past doesn't mean we have to be victims our entire lives.

A victim is someone who suffers from a destructive injury. Jesus died on the cross so that we could be healed. We don't have to remain injured. There's healing with Jesus. With the help of God, we can change and be whole. We can change our mindsets and habits. We can even change the way we see things by aligning our thoughts with what God says about us.

If the devil did something to me in my past, it's a choice to allow him to continue to do it repeatedly and bleed into my future. I can choose to put a halt to it, knowing I will have victory with Jesus. It's not too late to have the best life we can have. The devil wants us to doubt, give up and blame people. God wants us to press through, trust Him and give Him the glory at the victory line. There's hope and victory with Jesus!

LIFE LESSON: We can go from victim to victory. We may have been set back, but that doesn't have to hold us back. If we keep our eyes on Jesus, we'll not only *see* the finish line, but *experience the victory*.

MY PRAYER: Thank You, Lord, that my circumstances have no authority over my life. You're the Prince of hope and I put my trust and hope in You and You alone. My future is *secure* in Your hands. If I keep my eyes on You, You will lead me to the finish line.

HIS PROMISE:
"Though he falls, he will not be overwhelmed, for the LORD is holding his hand." — Psalm 37:24

"I'm not saying that I have this all together, that I have it made. But I am well on my way, reaching out for Christ, who has so wondrously reached out for me. Friends, don't get me wrong: By no means do I count myself an expert in all of this, but I've got my eye on the goal, where God is beckoning us onward—to Jesus. I'm off and running, and I'm not turning back."
— Philippians 3:14 MSG

What Will Others Think

"But blessed is the one who trusts in the Lord, whose confiden~
— Jeremiah 17:7

> *When we're secure in who we are because of who Jesus is in us, we realize we have all we need.*

Over the years when I would experience hardship, I allowed the devil to whisper lies of failure into my ear. The biggest lie the enemy would whisper was, "What will others think?" What I've learned over the years is they think, "Wow. She has struggles just like I do." Oddly enough, our problems bring encouragement to others. They let them know they're not alone.

It's not *having* the problem that encourages others, it's their *observation* of trusting Jesus. As we endure the battle, people take notice. It's trusting without yielding to the pressure that brings God glory. It demonstrates Jesus is bigger than our problems at hand. More importantly, it lets those who aren't believers have hope when they see our victory in Jesus despite our hardships.

When we're concerned with what people think, we allow the devil to bring insecurity to create doubt, and ultimately, stop our victory. Insecurity is nothing more than lack — lack of confidence, lack of truth and lack of self-worth.

Image is a global problem that brings insecurity. How our bodies look, our marriages appear, how well we've raised our children, our career status and our financial successes are all images that project concern about what people think.

When we're secure in *who* we are because of who Jesus is in us, we realize we have all we need. Matthew 6:34 clearly instructs us *not* to worry. Worry is defined as "torment to oneself with disturbing thoughts." When we worry about what others think, it brings unnecessary agony. Security in Jesus allows us not to care what others think.

I'm not suggesting having a haughty spirit, but confidence in Jesus. It *only* matters what Jesus says and thinks about who we are. When we go from worrying about what people think to trusting Jesus, is when we become secure and confident in the truth of what we know.

My position is to trust Jesus with my circumstances. Jesus sits on the right side of the throne of God interceding for us daily. Jesus is the defender of the brethren; Satan is the accuser of the brethren. As long as my actions demonstrate the love of Jesus and my beliefs the truth of Jesus, it doesn't matter what others think.

The people who often question us in the beginning are the same people who eventually come to us in the end for answers and prayer in their times of need. On the other side of our problem is the victory that will bring hope to lead others to their own victories.

LIFE LESSON: The more we grow and develop in the truth of the Word, the less we'll be concerned what others think. Consistency in our actions and beliefs will lead others to victory. When it's all said and done, the only thing people will be thinking is what an awesome God we serve.

MY PRAYER: Dear Lord, help me to remember the most important thing in life is not what people think, but the truth of who You are and what You've already done for me. Thank You for setting me free to be who You created me to be. Amen.

HIS PROMISE:
"Then you will know the truth, and the truth will set you free."
— John 8:32

"Therefore do not worry about tomorrow, for tomorrow will worry about itself. Each day has enough trouble of its own." — Matthew 6:34

Right Thinking

"Do not conform to the pattern of this world, but be transformed by the renewing of your mind. Then you will be able to test and approve what God's will is—His good, pleasing and perfect will." — Romans 12:2

> *What goes in our hearts will eventually be manifested in our lives.*

Years ago, I suffered the pain of betrayal in my previous marriage. The image of this other woman with my husband dominated my thoughts. In return, it controlled my feelings, days and life.

Continually, I rehearsed all the bad things I could imagine and how they'd affect my future. I meditated on these negative thoughts day and night, even to the point of becoming a detriment to my health.

If I ever want to have a life with intentional purpose, I've learned that I must *intentionally* put Scriptures in my heart. The devil *deliberately* fills our hearts and minds with the negative. If we let it, our focus will be on the negative. However, God wants us to *intentionally* place His Word and truth in our hearts and minds so that we can focus on His goodness.

If we neglect God's Word, which is good news, from entering our minds and hearts, we'll begin to adopt human reasoning and focus on the negative the world displays. God's goodness overpowers the worlds' ugliness.

When we guard our hearts with God's truth, God will guard our lives with His goodness. What we allow our minds to think about will eventually reveal the lives we're living. When we fill our minds with Christ-like thoughts, we'll live lives that are Christ-like. What I allow my mind to think about is a choice and my choice alone, which requires discipline. Even amid betrayal, the more I chose to guard my thoughts, the more I began to see I'm going to be alright. God has a future planned for us all, and it'll be good.

What goes in our hearts will eventually be manifested in our lives. Out of the abundance of our hearts is what is produced in our lives. All thoughts have a price. Good thoughts are seeds that produce value; however, bad thoughts are seeds that produce destruction.

The truth of God's Word that we meditate on will reveal the truth of the lives we choose to live. If we want to live lives of excellence, we must *intentionally choose* to think excellent thoughts. The results of good thinking are worth the effort. When I began to change my thoughts, it eventually changed who I became in Christ and the life I've lived.

LIFE LESSON: If I find my life in a place where I'm not satisfied, I've found my thoughts weren't thoughts that would produce satisfaction. If I want to think right, it's necessary to know God's truth, so I can live the excellent life Jesus died to give me.

MY PRAYER: Thank You, Lord, that today I have a choice to honor You with my thoughts. I choose to meditate on Your thoughts for my life. I'll decide to reject ugly thoughts and release them with Your truth. Help me to discipline my thought life so my life will reveal Your goodness. Amen.

HIS PROMISE:
"May these words of my mouth and this meditation of my heart be pleasing in your sight, Lord, my Rock, and my Redeemer." — Psalm 19:14

"As a man thinks in his heart, so is he." — Proverbs 23:7

Better Than Yesterday

"And the LORD restored the fortunes of Job when he prayed for his friends: also the LORD gave Job twice as much as he had before." — Job 42:10

> *The only thing that Jesus wants us to do with yesterday is learn from it and do better tomorrow.*

The devil wants us to think that the best is behind us; however, God has the best in front of us. There should never be a day when we wake up and today is lesser than yesterday. It's easy to get caught in the trap of yesterday. The Bible says Jesus is the same yesterday, today and forever.

His plans and purpose for our lives never change. He plans to prosper us in everything, including our health, well-being and finances. The only thing that Jesus wants us to do with yesterday is learn from it and do better tomorrow. I've found wisdom learns from yesterday while it's still today.

At night before I go to bed, I reflect on my day. I ask the Lord if I was a good steward of my day, my mouth and my actions. When I ask the Lord ahead of time to forgive me for any wrongdoings today, I'm able to wake up refreshed tomorrow with no regrets.

The devil wants us to live in the past with no hope for our future. I've learned that each step of our past paves the way for our future. My days of sorrow have made me appreciate my days of joy.

Zechariah 4:10 says, "Do not despise these small beginnings, for the LORD rejoices to see the work begin." In my former days of yesterday, I lost my home in a fire, my family to illness and my marriage to betrayal, but my God is *bigger* than my yesterday.

Today is bigger, fuller and richer in the Lord. No matter how far away we've strayed, how low we are or how much we've lost, God is near and will restore everything that was lost in our yesterdays and make life bigger and better today.

LIFE LESSON: Today may appear meaningless. We may feel lost and forgotten. But if we hang on and keep believing, God will reveal how meaningful and significant yesterday was for the lives we're living today.

MY PRAYER: Thank You, Lord, that I will not despise where I am today. You're faithful to take the fragments of my life and make them whole. You *will* restore my life bigger and better than yesterday. Amen.

HIS PROMISE:
"His possessions also were 7,000 sheep, 3,000 camels, 500 yokes of oxen, 500 female donkeys, and very many servants, and that man was the greatest of all the men of the east." — Job 1:3

"The LORD blessed the latter days of Job more than his beginning, and he had 14,000 sheep and 6,000 camels and 1,000 yoke of oxen and 1,000 female donkeys." — Job 42:12

Circumstances Are Temporary

"He has made everything beautiful in its time.
He has also set eternity in the human heart,
yet no one can fathom what God has done from beginning to end."
— Ecclesiastes 3:11

> Don't make a
> permanent decision
> in a temporary
> situation.

Years ago, the Lord spoke a truth to me, which has sustained my life. After a devastating divorce in 2000, my close friends and family suggested I move from my then current home into a smaller, more manageable home.

My former husband and I had just built our *dream home* on four acres — a beautiful piece of property. A few months later after moving into our dream home, all hell and havoc broke loose in my life. My 35-year-old sister's unexpected death was more than I could handle; however, a few short months later, the end of my marriage was more than I could bare.

The property was breathtaking; however, it required too much maintenance for a single, working female. In the process of the pressures regarding my life, the Lord spoke to me and said, "Don't make a *permanent decision* in a *temporary situation.*"

I've always kept those words close to my heart and remembered the wisdom in those powerful words. I've found that when life comes hurling at me in all directions, with unexpected events, it throws the direction I was going off course.

The pressure we put on ourselves pressures us to make decisions that are usually not in the best interest of our long-term welfare. When tragedy or tribulation presents itself, it seems everyone has an opinion for our lives. However, it's important to keep in mind that most people have the best intentions, but the One who has the *greatest* intentions and wisdom is the *Most High Jesus*, our Lord and Savior.

Honestly, I didn't have peace about moving. I felt like I would be letting the devil win. Why should he take my marriage *and* my home? When it's the right decision, the Lord will always give you His peace, prompting you to go forward. The Lord would have given me the desire to move, but that wasn't the case.

Against all odds and what appeared the right thing to do, I stayed. On Saturdays, it took seven hours' worth of mowing, but it was worth the battle to do what I felt the Lord was telling me to do. I was obedient and refused to make a permanent decision of a temporary situation. I knew deep inside there was a purpose *bigger* than myself to stay and occupy. Often, the purpose for a decision is revealed step by baby step as we move forward in obedience.

A few years later, they discovered oil and gas on my acreage and drilled a pipe through my property. As a result, I received royalties, which were beyond what I expected and more significant than most people in my area. In the meantime, I met someone with 100 acres who wasn't getting close to what my four acres were paying. By God's grace, we're still drawing royalties to this day. Even though it was a stretch to stay, God showed me that He would make up the difference.

At the time, I thought that was my sole purpose for keeping the property. My daughter was in college at the time. Little did I know that years later, she would get married and have eight children. Due to a turn of events — ordained by God — she and her husband sold their home, and moved into this special sanctuary of a home to raise their children on a property that was made for children to run, have freedom and enjoy life. What an awesome God we serve.

God's vision for our lives goes beyond our temporary circumstances. When things look upside down, remember that God has a plan. His plan sees beyond today. His plan is for our future.

LIFE LESSON: Our circumstances are subject to change. Today may present the unexpected, but if we trust God with our temporary situation, He'll take what looks like a mess and make it His ministry.

MY PRAYER: Thank You, Lord, for reminding me that You wrote my life story at the exact moment you created me. You knew what my life would hold from the beginning, and you see the end of my story. Help remind me that You have a beautiful future for me. Amen.

HIS PROMISE:
"'For I know the plans I have for you,'" declares the Lord, "'plans to prosper you and not to harm you, plans to give you hope and a future.'"
— Jeremiah 29:11

Step It Up

*"But as it is written: 'Eye hath not seen, nor ear heard,
neither have entered into the heart of man the things which
God hath prepared for them that love Him.'"* — 1 Corinthians 2:9

> *God can't promote
> our lifestyle to the
> next level, with our
> mind in the way.*

Over the years, I've learned you can't go to a new level in an old way of thinking. If I want my life to come up higher, my thinking must come up higher as well. Many times, God wanted to promote my life to the next level, but my thinking held me back.

When God brought my husband into my life — the man He had prepared to be my mate who I'd believed for years would manifest — I almost missed my promotion by my old mindset. To set something means "to place someone or something in a particular position" and you don't move it. It's set.

When we set our minds on what's familiar, we never step into all that God knows. Almost immediately, my husband-to-be knew I was the one who God had prepared for him to spend the rest of his life. He heard the voice of God, promptly obeyed without hesitation and told me, "I was the one."

When we allow our spirits to overrule our minds, then we're promoted in life. It's not mind over matter; it's *spirit over mind*. On the other hand, I had a mindset that this could not be; it was too soon. God doesn't rush. At the time, my mom was sick and lived out of state. She hadn't even met him. Thoughts raced through my mind, such as "the time is wrong" and "what if my children follow my example and think it's okay to rush in relationships." The list went on and on.

God can't promote our lives to the next level with our minds in the way. In the first place, God doesn't operate with our minds. He operates in the *spiritual realm*. He has accomplished in the Spirit everything in advance before we were born. The moment we took our first breath, He finished our lives in that exact moment. That is mind-boggling, but true. We'll never know what God has *already* prepared for our lives without getting in His Word. It is essential to get the Word from our minds and into our hearts.

When our minds begin to agree with His Word, our spirits will be able to comprehend His deep love for us. God's love will take us beyond where we've ever been before and will get us beyond the lives we're currently living.

If we want to experience life with the fullness of all that God has prepared and desire to go to the next level, we must be willing to get our minds out of the way and make room for God to do it His way.

LIFE LESSON: If I want my life to step up for promotion, I must step up my thinking. There's no way to get past where I am if I don't get past my old way of thinking.

MY PRAYER: Lord, help me to keep my mind on things above. Help me get my old way of doing things, my old way of thinking and old memories out of the way so that You can do new things in my life. Amen.

HIS PROMISE:
"Set your minds on things above, not on earthly things."— Colossians 3:2

"For my thoughts are not your thoughts, neither are your ways my ways, saith the Lord. For as the heavens are higher than the earth, so are my ways higher than your ways, and my thoughts than your thoughts."— Isaiah 55:8-10

Fear

"Fear not, for I am with you; be not dismayed, for I am your God;
I will strengthen you; I will help you,
I will uphold you with my righteous right hand."
— Isaiah 49:10

> *The devil's master plan is to disguise our circumstances to appear worse than they are so that we'll fear the outcome of our lives.*

As a child, at the young age of seven, I lived in Taiwan. My parents were out for the evening and our sitter was with my brothers and me. As I went into the kitchen to get a glass of milk, there standing before me was a man all dressed in black clothing, black gloves and a black ski mask pulled over his face to disguise himself. He had cut through the glass screen door and entered to rob our home. I screamed at the top of my lungs and he ran out the back door.

I believe at that moment in my life fear entered my heart and began to control my child-like mind. The devil's master plan is to disguise our circumstances to appear worse than they are so we will fear the outcome of our lives. Over and over, I thought about that image in my mind. Fear often begins with a single thought and causes us to start our thoughts with 'what ifs.' What if this happens again? What if I don't have enough money? What if I never find the right person for me? What if God is mad at me?

Fear is a tool of the devil, meant to draw us away from God and His vision for our lives. The earlier the devil can begin to torment our minds, the more control he can gain over our thoughts. From that moment on, fear was a powerful weapon that took control over my life.

Shortly after this incident, I began fearing thunder and lightning storms. The fear gripped me. The thunder didn't bother me, but I feared that the lightning would strike and blind my eyesight. What a strange thing for a child to be afraid of — not the loud bang of the thunder, but the loss of my sight. I truly would bury my face in the pillow and turn my back away from the window. This fear lasted even through high school.

How ironic looking back that in my young age the devil knew I would have God-inspired vision to advance His Kingdom. He made me fear the loss of vision. The devil knew that if the eyes of my understanding were enlightened and I was able to grasp the hope of God's calling for my life that he (the devil) would lose the power of control over me. Fear followed me into my adult life. I noticed that I followed a cycle of a fear-dominated life. Fear attracts and breeds fear.

As a result, I attracted men who could control me by fear and dictate my life with fear. At a young age, I ended up in a physically-abusive relationship. After that ended, I went on to another physically-abusive relationship, which was worse than the previous one. I thought I'd broken the cycle, but ended up in the ultimate verbally-abusive relationship that I thought would kill the last of my self-worth.

The devil is on duty 24 hours a day to strip us of our self-worth. I had no idea why I ended up in these relationships because I loved the Lord and wanted to please Him. They *appeared* to be good men; however, I learned that fear clouds vision to see God's truth. Fear destroys the perception of reality.

The very foundation of fear is based on the loss. Instead of trusting God for the right man, the fear of no man caused me to be with any man. Fear keeps us blinded from seeing that God has a hand-picked person *just for us*. Fear settles for less. Fear means "a distressing emotion aroused by impending danger of evil or pain." Whether the threat is real or imagined, the fear is real to us. There is a saying that 'my perception is my reality.'

The devil wants us to think that his perception is reality, which is not the truth. God's Word is the highest form of reality and truth. I've learned to not allow my feelings to dictate my emotions by what I see and feel.

If we allow it, our feelings will drag us up and down and back around the same mountain over and over. It's a constant battle to not allow our feelings to control the position of our lives. I may not feel worthy, but that doesn't change the fact God says, "I am worthy." I may not feel healed, but that doesn't change the fact that God's Word says, "I am healed."

Over the years, I've discovered that it's up to me to take control. I can *choose* to be controlled by the Spirit of God or I can choose to be controlled by fear. Fear produces torment while God's Spirit produces peace. I've tried both and have decided, after much deliberation and experience – that the righteous rule of peace reigning in my life is where all victory is found.

LIFE LESSON: Fear may bring torment, but God's perfect love casts out fear. The devil may try and strike, but God has stripped him of all authority. The quicker we make a decision to break free, the quicker we'll experience true and lasting victory in Christ.

MY PRAYER: Thank You, Lord, that I'm free from the spirit of fear. The truth of Your power and love will loose me from the bondage the devil has tried to hold over me. I'm thankful for Your peace. I choose to replace the devil's thoughts with Your thoughts and words You sing over me. I'm free. I'm truly free. Your perfect love has set me free to live my life in victory. Amen.

HIS PROMISE:
"There is no fear in love. But perfect love drives out fear because fear has to do with punishment. The one who fears is not made perfect in love."
— 1 John 4:18

"And the peace of God, which passes all understanding, shall keep your hearts and minds through Christ Jesus." — Philippians 4:7

I Decided Yesterday

*"Therefore, do not be anxious for tomorrow, for tomorrow will care for itself.
Each day has enough trouble of its own."* — Matthew 6:34

> *We can decide to give victory to the devil and agree what we see is our final outcome, or we can give victory to Jesus in spite of what we see.*

In my life, I've faced many tough decisions. Having been a young, single parent, I had to decide I would be a successful mother and provider for my baby. Losing a brother at 29 years of age to a car crash, a sister at 35 years of age to diabetes, a mother to cancer and a father to chronic obstructive pulmonary disease, I had to decide that I wouldn't let that weaken my faith in God as my healer.

Having a (previously) failed marriage, I had to decide that God didn't fail me. As a single woman for 10 years, I had to decide to believe God had the perfect mate — hand-picked just for me. When finances were less than needed, I had to decide to believe God was sufficient to meet all my needs. When my children were going through (and still go through) difficult situations, I have to decide that I'll not me moved.

Through these challenges and trials, I've come to the conclusion that if I resolve my controversies and struggles in advance, it helps eliminate torment in the future. I've learned to determine and settle in advance that I'll trust Jesus with the outcomes. We have to be persuaded with no reservation that Jesus is working out all things for our good, regardless of how it may appear.

One of the definitions of decide is "to solve or conclude (a question, controversy, or struggle) by giving victory to one side." Wow, how powerful is that. We can decide to give victory to the devil and agree that what we see is our final outcome, or we can give victory to Jesus in spite of what we see.

1 John 5:4 says, "For everyone of God overcomes the world, even our faith." As a child of God, we defeat this evil world, as we achieve victory through our faith. Our faith in Jesus is the victory that has conquered our tragedies, heartbreaks and disappointments.

If God is for us, nothing can come against us. We have permanent victory in Christ. When this world appears to be economically and socially devastated, void of hope for the future, I've decided to trust Jesus, who's the redeemer of it all.

LIFE LESSON: It's not always easy to trust God at all times. However, when we decide in advance that no matter what happens tomorrow, no matter how hard it is to understand, and no matter how bad it may appear, we'll trust God with today and find comfort with whatever tomorrow may bring.

MY PRAYER: Thank You, Lord, that You are God. You are my healer, You are my comforter and You are my redeemer for every need in every situation. I trust You today for whatever tomorrow brings. Amen.

HIS PROMISE:
"For I know that my Redeemer lives, and He shall stand at last on the earth." — Job 19:26

"Trust in the LORD with all your heart, And do not lean on your understanding. In all your ways, acknowledge Him, And He will make your paths straight." — Proverbs 3:5-6

"Therefore, my dear brothers and sisters, stand firm. Let nothing move you. Always give yourselves fully to the work of the Lord, because you know that your labor in the Lord is not in vain." — 1 Corinthians 15:58

The Rest of the Story

"The glory of this latter house shall be more splendid than of the former, saith the Lord of hosts: and in this place will I give you peace, saith the Lord of the host." — Haggai 2:9

> *When someone leaves us against our will, we have to understand that his part of our story is over, but there's always more to our story.*

Twenty-two years ago, I walked into my home. As I entered the closet, my former husband's side of the closet had been cleaned out. It was totally empty. Divorce papers were lying neatly in my makeup drawer. When someone leaves us against our will, we have to understand that his part of our story is over, but there's always more to our story.

When we have something happen and are caught off guard, God is not. Not ever. Isaiah 52:12 says, "He who goes before you is our rear guard." He has our back, sees where we've been and where we're going. He knows the end from the beginning. When someone exits our lives, his part of our story is over. But God has a new chapter with a new title for our lives titled 'the rest of the story.'

Although there are always two sides to every story, *God's* story is all that matters. He has written the final chapter. Regardless of what happens in the middle, the end of the story is already written. The future is finished.

When my former husband left, his part in my life was over, but my life was not over. The longer I wallowed in grief and self-pity, the longer it took me to move into my prepared place of happiness. It takes two things to receive the promises of God — faith and patience. God will *never* fail us, but He won't bring to pass what we can't receive. He will lovingly and patiently wait until we're ready.

Our hearts have to be open to receive a new season. A closed

29

heart can never receive the fullness of love. When a door is shut, we have no way of seeing what's on the inside. When a heart is closed, it shuts out every blessing that flows from God. I was single for
10 years, partly due to the severity of my heart condition, and my inability to see, to receive. However, God still fulfilled the promise of the deep desire of my heart. He brought me a godly man who would be faithful to pursue Him and faithful to lead and love me.

By the grace of God, my life today exceeds anything I could ever comprehend in my former life. God promises our latter lives will be greater than the former. The Bible tells a story of a wealthy man named Job. The beginning of this book sounded like a fairytale. It tells of a man who was blameless and upright. He feared God and shunned the devil. However, he seemingly lost everything — his servants, animals and all of his offspring.

As if that was not bad enough, he also was afflicted from head to toe with painful sores. However, that was not the end of Job's story. The Lord blessed his latter days greater than his former. He went on to have over 20,000 animals, 10 children and many grandchildren.

Job 8:7 says, "Though your beginning was small, yet your latter end would increase abundantly." God told Job that although he suffered and thought he had lost everything worth living for, He would restore his account better than it started. The same applies to us today.

Although our beginnings may appear small, our days ahead will greatly increase. Whether it's been one day, two days or 20 years, it's never too late to be happy. God *will* finish the rest of our story today if we're genuinely ready to believe and receive it for tomorrow.

LIFE LESSON: If someone or something exits our lives, God has already prepared a place of happiness to enter. Our life is not over; the rest of our story is about to begin.

MY PRAYER: Lord, help me to trust You in times of despair. I know You have written my story before I was born. Help me to never forget that You have more for me than my eyes can see. You can restore anything lost, exceedingly abundantly above what I could imagine. Amen.

HIS PROMISE:
"Though your beginning was small, yet your latter end would increase abundantly." — Job 8: 7

"Now to Him who is able to do exceedingly abundantly above all that we ask or think, according to the power that works in us."- Ephesians 3:20

Change Starts in the Heart

"Above all else, guard your heart, for everything you do flows from it."
— Proverbs 4:23

When it's settled in our hearts, it's in heaven.

Anytime I need a radical change in my life, I've discovered it was necessary for a radical heart change. Not only is the heart a vital organ that keeps us alive, it's also a vital organ for change. Change must first start in the heart.

You may be familiar with the phrase, "The heart of a matter," which means it's the innermost central part of anything. When it's settled in our hearts, it's settled in heaven.

Over the years, I've found the key to any change is finding out what God says about the matter and then getting myself in agreement with His Word in my heart. His Word is truth, it's settled and it's forever the same. God's Word isn't fickle or uncertain; it's settled, determined, fixed, sure and immovable. God will *never* move off what He's said. He says we're blessed with *all* spiritual blessings, we're chosen, we're heirs, we're His workmanship and we're partakers of His promises.

However, it's *our* job to receive His promises into our hearts. It's not necessary to determine our next step, but we do need to determine our next heartbeat with God. It's either going to beat in agreement *with* God or have the offbeat of the world. The world's way is offbeat from God's way. I need to get myself in agreement with what God says. When my heart says, "Yes Lord, I Believe," God says, "Yes it is done." Religion says *do*; Jesus says *finished*.

Jesus doesn't want us to *do* anything; He only wants *our agreement.* When God created our lives, He finished it in the same breath. It brings comfort knowing that everything we need God has already determined for us in His Word. He has determined our victory; we must determine our hearts to agree.

Proverbs 4:20-23 instructs us to pay close attention to God's instruction. "Let not my sayings depart from your eyes; keep them amid your heart. For they are life to those who find them, and health to all their flesh. Keep your heart with all diligence; for out of your heart are the issues of life." He knows all the things that are vital, for our lives flow from our hearts. Our love, emotions, energy and confidence offload from our hearts.

So when I find it necessary for radical change, I prepare myself for radical heart surgery. As in all surgery, there's pain in the beginning. However, once the surgery is complete, there's a new freedom to live and move in a way that you were unable to do before.

LIFE LESSON: When I find "life" weighing me down, I immediately look at the condition of my heart. When I exercise my heart by exercising it in God's Word, not only do I stretch my spiritual muscles, my heart becomes stronger to do all that's necessary to accomplish the change that God desires.

MY PRAYER: Thank You, Lord, that You are concerned about the condition of my heart. Help me to stay in Your Word, so my heart stays beating in one accord with Yours. I desire change and will do what is necessary. Amen.

HIS PROMISE:
"Forever, O LORD, your word is settled in heaven."— Psalm 118:89

"My flesh and my heart may fail, but God is the strength of my heart and my portion forever." — Psalm 73:26

God Will Part Our "Red Sea"

"And Moses stretched out his hand over the sea, and the LORD caused the sea to go back by a strong east wind all that night and made the dry sea land, and the waters were divided."— Exodus 14:21

> *When it looks like our situations are hopeless and circumstances are "dead," never to be revived, God's ready to breathe life into the problem.*

God will make way for the redeemed to pass over. When things appear to be dried up in our lives, God will cause living water to flow again. When life seems to be overwhelming, God will cause the troubled waters to dry up. I've been through desperate times where it appeared that there was no way out. I can remember being trapped in a physically- abusive relationship, fearing no way of escape.

The Bible says hope deferred makes the heart sick (Proverbs 13:12). Satan wants to steal our hope. When it looks like our situations are hopeless and circumstances are "dead," never to be revived, God's ready to breathe life into the problem.

When the Israelites were released from under the rule of Pharaoh's heavy hand of slavery and bondage, they rejoiced for their long-awaited freedom. It amazes me when we've been set free, how quickly we forget we've been redeemed.

The same God who redeemed us will *not* leave us. He didn't set us free to send us back to the place we came from. Only the devil can try to make us think that He's sending us back. If we're not careful, we can quickly take our appreciation and turn it into apprehension. As a result, we begin to anticipate adversity and misfortune, and fear future trouble.

When we've been delivered from bondage, we want to focus on what God has already done, not on what *might* be to come. We need to forget our past and focus on our future in Christ. However, we don't need to forget the past that God has delivered us out of.

We may not be exactly where we need to be. However, if we focus on where we came from, we'll see that we've already made major steps of victory.

The Israelites took their freedom and began to complain about their new circumstances. It wasn't long before they were backed up against the Red Sea with Pharaoh's army surrounding them.

When we complain, it blinds us to what God is doing and causes us to focus on everything we *feel* He is *not* doing. When we're backed up against a wall, with no way out and nowhere to go, God wants to show us once again that He's not only *the* way, but the *only* way. No army can stop the power of God's mighty hand to part our "Red Sea."

Recently, I've been reminding myself of that. Life frequently shows no mercy, but thank God His mercies are fresh every morning. We don't have to know what God will do amid circumstances or how He'll do it. However, we do need to trust that He will do it in His timing.

When we're backed up against the "Red Sea" and Satan's army is behind us, rejoice because God has the power to part that Red Sea for us to walk across into victory.

LIFE LESSON: No army in hell can hold back the hand of Almighty God to part the rough stormy sea for us to walk across to the other side in victory. Therefore, be encouraged. Your "Red Sea" will part.

MY PRAYER: Thank You, Lord, that You will never lose the power to part our Red Seas. There's not one thing in life that overwhelms You. You are mighty and strong, and never grow weary. Your hand isn't too short that it can't reach out and save us in this world. Amen.

HIS PROMISE:

"Let the redeemed of the LORD say so, whom he has redeemed from the hand of the enemy." — Psalm 107:2

"Whom you have redeemed by your great power and brought out of Egypt with a mighty hand." — Deuteronomy 9:26

Beyond What We Know

"Great is our Lord and abundant in power;
His understanding is beyond measure." — Psalm 147:5

> *If I stay within the boundaries God has placed around my life, He'll personally take me beyond any place that I could have imagined for my life.*

The devil wants to unleash all boundaries from our lives. There was a time in my life I ignored boundaries, which would ultimately put me in uncomfortable positions. Saying no when I should've said yes. Saying yes when I should've said no. Staying awake when I should've been asleep. Going to sleep when I should've been awake. Working when I should've been resting and resting when I should've been working.

Anytime I have gone beyond what I knew was the right thing to do, I've ended up in situations where I ultimately didn't know what to do. Therefore, I've learned that if I stay in the boundaries God has placed around my life, He will personally take me beyond any place that I could've imagined for my life. Beyond means "more than; over and above." When I trust the boundaries God has drawn for my life, I find He takes me farther, more than and in excess of and over and above where I could've gone on my own. God wants to stretch us to go beyond our own thinking and ability.

When we want to give up, He wants to push us beyond. When life presents hardships, He'll stretch us beyond. But beyond where? Beyond where we are, beyond where we've been and beyond where we can see.

When I was a young, single parent and barely making it, He took me beyond where I could've ever imagined for my life. God is able to go beyond *any* dream we could dream for ourselves. Along the way, God has shown me He always has *more* in store. No matter how long we've lived, how long we've been married, how long we've been waiting and no matter how big the dream, He *always* has more.

Yesterday, I was single, broke and in a season of barely enough. Today, I'm married to my "gift" (husband) from God, enjoying the abundantly blessed life He has given me. God has a life planned beyond our imaginations when we stay within the boundaries of His Love.

LIFE LESSON: When we let go of what we know and trust God with His boundaries, He will take us beyond where we've ever dreamed we could go.

MY PRAYER: Thank You, Lord, that You are able to provide beyond what we could ever provide for ourselves. You see what we can't see. Thank You for a life of fulfillment, enjoyment and contentment. Amen.

HIS PROMISE:
"Now unto him, that can do exceeding abundantly above all that we ask or think, according to the power that works in us." — Ephesians 3:20

"Oh, the depth of the riches of the wisdom and knowledge of God! How unsearchable his judgments, and his paths beyond tracing out." — Romans 11:33 (NIV)

It's Our Choice

*"This day I call the heavens and the earth as witnesses against you
that I have set life and death, blessings and curses.
Now choose life so that you and your children may live."*
— Deuteronomy 30:19

> *I must choose to live a life based on the truth of God's Word, not my feelings.*

If we can make the right choices while still hurting, we'll have victory over our pain. We have to *choose* to forgive while we're still hurting. We have to *choose* to give when we've been taken advantage of. We have to *choose* to love in the midst of people mistreating us.

We have to *choose* to keep moving forward when everything screams quit. Our choices determine our lives. The Bible says, "I set before you blessings and curses, life and death. Choose life." It's a choice. I must *choose* to live a life based on the truth of God's Word, not my feelings.

When I was a single parent, my choice to not give up and press beyond my feelings changed the course of not only my life, but that of my children and my childrens' children's destinies.

Feelings are a part of our souls, but our feelings are *not* to run our lives. We're not to bow down and give in to our feelings, but we're to bow down to God and submit to His Word. Feelings will *never* tell us the truth; they'll only reveal to us how we feel. How we feel is *not* the truth of how it is. Emotions don't determine the lives God has for us.

The only thing that determines our lives are the choices we make. God gave us all the right to choose. He made us all equal. Our color, social status, circumstances and/or career don't determine the lives we live. It's the *choices* we make. Therefore, I chose to live the life Jesus died to give me, which sets me free.

LIFE LESSON: Our lives are a reflection of the choices we make. We can live lives of good choices or we can choose to exist. If I want to live a good life, I must determine that it's up to me to choose to live it.

MY PRAYER: Thank You, Lord, that today You help me make the right choices based on the truth of Your Word. Today, I'm determined not to live by how people treat me or how I feel, but by the truth of Your Word. I submit my feelings and bow down to You in the midst of how I feel. Please forgive me for yesterday and reveal to me Your plan for today. Amen.

HIS PROMISE:
"The thief does not come except to steal, and to kill, and to destroy. I have come that they may have life and that they may have it more abundantly." — John 10:10

"Jesus answered, 'I am the way and the truth and the life. No one comes to the Father except through me.'" — John 14:6

It Is Finished

"Being confident in this, He who began a good work in you will carry it on to completion until the day of Christ Jesus." — Philippians 1:6

> *We're not here to finish His work, but to finish our race.*

Through my many struggles and self-effort, I've learned that Jesus' success on the cross swallowed up any failures in my life. If we genuinely believe we'll finish our race, we must believe Jesus did a finished work on the cross on our behalf.

We can't fully believe in Jesus and trust in ourselves. We must get to the point where we trust that Jesus did it *all*. We're not here to finish His work, but to finish our race. Sometimes the very thing we so desperately want will be the same thing that becomes an obstacle in our race.

Obstacles are defined as "something that obstructs or hinders our progress." I can remember desperately wanting to find love. I never had a father's love, so in my desperation, I tried to fill a void only Jesus could fill. I went from relationship to relationship, all the while trying to run my race.

Through trying to find love, I lost sight of my race. I got distracted, and eventually, I was lost, losing all vision for my race. In all actuality, I was running in the opposite direction of my race. I needed to be running *into* the arms of Jesus, not running into the arms of men.

After many years of failed relationships and a broken heart, I finally surrendered all. I was exhausted, tired and finally done. I remember thinking — "That's it, I'm done. No more."

God was probably rejoicing, saying "Finally, she's done. Now I can begin." When we end, God can begin. Nine months after I said, "I'm done," I said, "I do!" God presented my husband, a God-fearing man, who's truly a gift.

Now, I run my race with someone by my side. God already had my husband waiting; God was waiting on *me* to let go. It's only when we release our lives that God will release all *He* has for our lives.

Therefore, be encouraged that Jesus did it all. It is finished. Rest in Him and run *your* race with confidence.

LIFE LESSON: It is finished. What we start, God has already finished. When we're secure in Jesus, we'll spend more time fulfilling our destiny and less time fearing if it will ever arrive.

MY PRAYER: Thank You, Lord, that although there may be delays that hinder my race, You never lose sight of the victory line. Thank You that I can rest in Your finished work on the cross. Amen.

HIS PROMISE:
"When He had received the drink, Jesus said, 'It is finished.' With that, he bowed His head and gave up His Spirit." — John 19:30

"Let us throw off everything that hinders and the sin that so easily entangles. And let us run with perseverance the race marked out for us."
— Hebrews 12:1

Jesus Paid It All

"Then you will know the truth, and the truth will set you free."
— John 8:32

> The truth of Jesus
> penetrated through
> the deception of
> Buddha.

Recently, I went to the nail salon, but my normal nail technician was on vacation in Vietnam. I had a new woman do my nails. In our conversation, she shared with me how her husband had died of cancer and now she was a widow at a young age.

Her husband was an American and claimed to be a Christ-follower, although he attended the temple with her to pray to Buddha. In his last days, she went on her computer and googled how to bring comfort to a dying spouse in his final days.

Then she ran across a heading titled "Near Death Experience." She assumed it was someone who almost died. Perhaps she could find comfort in it for her husband. Little did she know those words would help her find comfort for eternity.

As she read on, it talked about someone who had died and met Jesus. It said that Jesus died for our sins and that He paid the price for our lives. She immediately was drawn in. As she continued to read, she had an unusual eagerness to learn more. She told me that when she read those words, she had a hunger in her heart to know more about this man named Jesus.

She was so surprised to read about such a man. With Buddha, he requires payment — there's a penalty for our sin. We must pay a price, and Buddha charges the sin to our account. She couldn't believe that a man named Jesus, whom she'd never met, would pay for her sins.

It was such an innocent picture of someone understanding the redemption story for the first time. How beautiful that a seed was planted to know a man named Jesus, because her god demanded payment for her sin. Our God *personally* paid for our sins in advance. What a powerful expression of His love for us.

Now, the Word of God was activated in her spirit and the truth of Jesus penetrated through the deception of Buddha. She said the hunger to know Jesus became so intense in her heart that she went to the temple and said, "Buddha, if you're real, hold me back from Jesus because everything in me wants to have Jesus in my heart." In stunned silenced, she said nothing happened.

How great is our God. No power in hell can hold back the love of Jesus. Since Buddha did nothing, she went home and asked Jesus into her heart. In that very moment, she was changed on the inside. She went on to lead her husband to the Lord before he died, and he went on to heaven.

God had a plan. Her husband was a millionaire and left her all his investments and savings. Her home was paid for and he made sure she was taken care of for the rest of her life. She sends most of her money back home to Vietnam because she said the poor need help from the blessed. She said, "It's not my money anyway. Everything I have belongs to God. I'll spend my life serving Him, since He lived His life to die for me."

Her pure love for Jesus has inspired me. The beautiful picture of how while we were yet sinners, Jesus knew us and loved us despite ourselves. Often when we're born into a Christian home, we can take the free gift of salvation for granted.

The profound impact the love of Jesus had on her life also impacted mine. I've had the honor and privilege of taking my new sister in Christ to the house of God. What a joy to watch this woman worship Jesus with such freedom and expressing her love to the Man who paid it all.

LIFE LESSON: The love of Jesus is a free gift. Although it cost us nothing, we need to be mindful that it cost Jesus everything, even His life. The most beautiful expression of our love is sharing His free gift with others. There's no devil in hell that can hold back the love of Jesus from setting us free.

MY PRAYER: Thank You, Lord, for the free gift of salvation. Help me to remember that Your sacrifice is a precious gift and expression of Your deep love for me. Amen.

HIS PROMISE:
"And Jesus said unto them, I am the bread of life: he that cometh to me shall never hunger; and he that believeth on me shall never thirst." — John 6:35

"For the wages of sin is death, but the free gift of God is eternal life in Christ Jesus our Lord." — Romans 6:23

Worship

"God is Spirit, and those who worship Him must worship in spirit and truth."
— John 4:24

True worship puts God above everything else.

Worship is an expression of honor or homage we pay to God. The words, "I Worship You Lord," sometimes carelessly rolls off the lips of many believers. True worship is revealed in the lives we live. It's not something we say; it's how we live.

Worship has many facets of expression. When I was a young believer, I didn't quite understand the meaning of worship. I've since learned that worship is something we *cultivate*. Cultivate means "to improve the growth of." As we grow in our relationship with Jesus, we grow in our understanding of how to worship in spirit and in truth.

Worship puts what we worship above anything else. I see so many people worship money, putting the dollar above family, integrity and ethics. True worship puts God *above* everything else, causing us to be conscious of God in everything we do.

We worship in thanksgiving amid circumstances being less than desired. In Romans 4:17, God calls the things that are not as though they are. We're not to call things that are as they are. We're to call things that shouldn't be as God intended them to be. We're not to call ourselves sick, but call sickness into the submission to God's Word and call ourselves healed. In His word, it says we're healed by the stripes Jesus bore to make us whole. We're not the sick *trying* to get well, but the redeemed of the Lord healed and made whole.

We're not to call debt lack, but call lack into the submission of God's Word. God is the great El Shaddai, not 'El Cheap O.' He's *more* than enough to meet all our needs. Paul tells us in Philippians 4:18, "My God, will met all my needs according to His riches." And this includes our finances. When we give God thanks in the midst of lack, we worship Him as *provider* — El Jireh.

In addition, we worship God in *praise*. We shouldn't give credit to ourselves in the midst of promotion, acceleration and good things happening in our lives, but we should give thanks to Him who lives and has His being, free to move and guide us in our lives.

We worship with *humility*. When we're promoted and humble ourselves and give all the glory to God (giving credit where credit is due), that's a form of worship. When we don't self-promote, but do what's right in secret, God *will* promote in public.

We worship by *repentance*. God tells us in His Word that any mountain that stands in our way, we have authority, in His name, to remove it. However, He goes on to say there's one condition. "When you stand praying, if you hold anything against anyone, forgive them, so that your Father in heaven may forgive you your sins" (Mark 11:25). When we ask forgiveness for sins of remission as well as omission (sins we're not aware of), we honor God and worship Him in humility.

We worship with our *money*. When we let go of the control of money from our hands, we release God's power to get His surplus of money into our hands. Money is the god of this world. When we turn over our money to God, it shows the God of *our* world is God almighty. He's our provider in the beginning and end of everything in our lives.

We worship by *serving others*. When we put others before ourselves, it's a form of worship to God. Matthew 20:28 says, "Just as the Son of Man did not come to be served, but to serve, and to give his life as a ransom for many." God almighty laid down His Son as an expression of His love. To lay our lives down and serve is one of the greatest expressions of worship.

John 13:34 says, "A new command I give you: 'Love one another, as I have loved you, so you must love one another. By this everyone will know that you are my disciples, if you love one another.'"

We worship by *giving*. When we give our money, time and resources to those in need, we worship God. God said He loves a cheerful giver. When we give our time, money and love (even to those who don't deserve it) without grumbling and complaining, it comes to heaven as a beautiful melody into the ears of God Almighty.

In essence, worship is not something we say, it's an expression of how we live. When we say, "We worship you Lord," we're really saying, "Everything I do, I do unto You."

LIFE LESSON: A life of worship isn't what we do, it's who we are. True worship is evident in the expression of the lives we're living.

MY PRAYER: Thank you Lord, that you are completely worthy of my worship. Teach me how to worship you in every aspect of my life, show me the areas where I have not yet put your above all else. Amen.

HIS PROMISE:
"Jesus answered, 'It is written: Worship the Lord your God and serve him only.'" — Luke 4:8

Focus

"Therefore, holy brothers, partners in a heavenly calling,
keep your focus on Jesus." — Hebrews 3:1

> The depth of our praise will determine the magnitude of our breakthrough.

Every night before I go to bed, I pick out my clothes for the next day. One particular night, I was looking for a white blouse with a large black stripe around the bottom. My clothes are coordinated by color, so I was in the black and white section. I slowly went through each blouse one at a time, but couldn't find it anywhere.

After I looked six or seven times, I went through them slowly one at a time with no success of finding it. In the end, I decided to wear something else. As I walked away from the closet, a thought occurred to me — I think that blouse may be black with a white stripe. I turned around, walked back in my closet and went through the section one more time and immediately found the blouse. The Lord instantly spoke to my heart and said, "This is what happens when you're in need of something and focused on the wrong thing. Your answer will be right in front of you all along, but because you're focused on the wrong thing you can't see it." It was right in front of me all along, but I was focusing on white and not black.

This is an example of a rhema word in due time. God's *always* speaking, but unfortunately, we're not the best in listening. We often have a need at hand, which diverts our eyes to desperately focus on our needs *instead* of Jesus. He's always the answer to every need. He meets of our needs. Always.

His Word says to seek God first and His way of doing things, and He'll personally take care of every need we have and add to our lives in ways we're not able to. God always has creative ways for provision. He brings us a mate, restores our marriages, finds us a new home and turns the hearts of our children back to Himself. When we focus on Jesus, He'll focus on *our* needs. The demands of life alone are too much for us, but it's not too much for God who created all things, and knows the beginning from the end.

At one point in my life, I had a situation that I was deeply concerned about. God once again reminded me to get my eyes *off* the problem, and *on* the answer. I heard Brother Jerry Savelle, a preacher to the nations, say, "The depth of our praise will determine the magnitude of our breakthrough. Needs can cause rumbling in our hearts and mouths, but praise will cause the enemy to halt."

Instead of magnifying our concerns by continually rehearsing them in our minds and speaking them out of our mouths, we should replace our concerns with God's truth. Nothing is impossible with God; He *will* meet all our needs with His Kingdom provision. No weapon formed against us, our families or careers will prosper. We have the wisdom of God and will make every decision concerning our lives with confidence and direction by the Spirit of God. When God is on our side and our focus is on Him, we can clearly see we're always on the winning side.

LIFE LESSON: The things we are most focused on will *always* navigate the direction our lives go. If we want to see things clearly, our eyes have to be clearly on Jesus. He's the answer to *every* equation.

MY PRAYER: Lord, help us keep our eyes focused on You so we don't make mistakes. You bring the answer to every equation, every time. You'll never let us down. Help us to keep our heads up and eyes fixed on You. Remind us that Your Word not only has power, but authority to override *any* situation that *looks* impossible. Amen.

HIS PROMISE:
"Because he has focused his love on me, I will deliver him. I will protect him because he knows my name. When he calls out to me, I will answer."
— Psalm 91:14-15

"My son, stay focused; listen to the wisdom I have gained; give attention to what I have learned about life so you may be able to make sensible judgments and speak with knowledge." — Proverbs 5:1-2

Revealed for a Reason

*"It is the glory of God to conceal a thing:
but the honor of kings is to search out a matter."* — Proverbs 25:2

> *God will use the mistakes of others to redirect the steps of our future.*

I've often learned that God will show us what's wrong and reveal what's right. Many times in ministry, friendship and business, I'd see disturbing things. It's disappointing to witness a lack of integrity, disrespect and dishonor from ones I'd respected.

Perhaps, someone you respect does something that hurts you or disappoints you. The higher you go in a position, the closer you are to people with authority. Likewise, the higher up you go, the more you see.

As a result, there're two things I've learned. First, people are just people, and there's a reason God is showing me. Everything Jesus allows us to see has a purpose. God isn't wasteful. He used the dirt of the ground to create man, so surely God will use the mistakes of others to redirect the steps of our future. Secondly, the more I grow in the Lord, the more He allows me to see. He'll reveal things not for criticism, but for revelation. What God reveals can revolutionize our lives.

Now, I understand character issues or things revealed in others aren't for me to judge, but for me to see and perceive the repercussion. Therefore, I'll not repeat the mistake in the future that which I'm experiencing now. God's merciful and wants us to succeed. So now, if I see anything disturbing, I ask the Lord, "What are You showing me and why?"

When I apply it to myself, it not only removes me from the 'judge's chair,' it puts me in a position to care and prepare for what lies ahead.

LIFE LESSON: God will reveal mistakes to us to avoid pain in our future. When we see something wrong today, it's an opportunity to get it right and not make the same mistake tomorrow.

MY PRAYER: Thank You, Lord, that You love me so much that You allow me to learn firsthand through others' mistakes. Help me use these opportunities as a time to pray, intercede and learn from them in my own life. Amen.

HIS PROMISE:

"These are the things God has revealed to us by his Spirit. The Spirit searches all things, even the deep things of God." — 1 Corinthians 2:10

"Fear them not therefore: for there is nothing covered, that shall not be revealed; and hid, that shall not be known." — Matthew 10:26

Step Into the Blessing

"The LORD shall command the blessing on you in your storehouses, and in all that you set your hand to; and he shall bless you in the land which the LORD your God gives you." — Deuteronomy 28:8

> *God will give in great quantities what we need when we need it and right on time.*

The Lord said He would cause the enemies that rise against us to be defeated. Even though they come against us in one way, they'll flee before us in seven ways. No weapon formed against our bodies, finances, homes, careers or families can come against us.

In Deuteronomy, God says that He'll command the blessing on all of our storehouses to which we set our hand to. When God commands the blessing, it'll perform in our lives. In today's vernacular, a storehouse is simply a source of abundant supply. He'll bless us in the place we stand. We may not have received the job promotion we needed, but God will bless us with where we are to meet our needs. It goes on to say in Deuteronomy that He will establish us, meaning He will cause us to be recognized and remain firm in our position.

He'll make us stable in an unstable world. The world may overlook us; however, God's in pursuit of us. It goes on to say that He'll grant us plenty of goods. Goods are defined as "anything in surplus, prosperity or possessions," which includes the fruit of our bodies (healthy, whole and healed), the increase of our livestock (increased wealth) and the produce of our ground (financial provision). His provision puts us in a position to give where we never need to take out a loan, which is a result of a surplus of prosperity.

As if that isn't enough to make us excited, God finishes His declaration by saying He *will* open up to us His good treasure to give us rain to our lands in its season. Rain means God will give in great quantities what we need, when we need it and right on time.

We certainly serve a timely God.

His favor will be poured down from heaven, showering us in the season we need it. I love the following statement — we will be the head and not the tail. You'll only be above.

We were meant to live *above* our circumstances, not beneath the life Jesus died to give us. When we recognize the blessing on our lives, the devil can't defeat us in our minds. Remember that no weapon can penetrate when the blessing of God is in our lives.

LIFE LESSON: God commanded His blessing on our lives; we only need to step into it. What God commands stands. We may not see it, but when we believe, we can rest assured the blessing of God is on the way.

MY PRAYER: Thank You, Lord, for commanding the blessing on our lives. Help us recognize the benefits You've placed in our lives and cause us to be firm and stable in our position. Amen.

HIS PROMISE:
"The LORD shall open unto thee his good treasure, the heaven to give the rain unto thy land in his season, and to bless all the work of thine hand: and thou shalt lend unto many nations, and thou shalt not borrow."
— Deuteronomy 28:12

"Bring the whole tithe into the storehouse, that there may be food in my house. Test me in this," says the LORD Almighty, "and see if I will not throw open the floodgates of heaven and pour out so much blessing that there will not be room enough to store it." — Malachi 3:10

Jesus "Out Shines" Buddha

"Let your light so shine before men that they may see your good works, and glorify your Father, which is in heaven." — Matthew 5:15

> *I've learned that people respond to Jesus by what they see, not by what we preach.*

Over the years, I've had numerous opportunities to allow my light of Jesus to shine. As Christians, we sometimes believe it might be intrusive to shine a bright light into the eyes of those who've sat in darkness for years. In 1992, I went to a new nail salon. Ricky, the owner, was from Cambodia, and the most joyful person.

His English was broken, but he always had a smile on his face and upbeat music playing. The salon was filled with the aroma of burning incense, and the display of his passion for his Buddha sat right in front of his station.

He was proud to display his god front and center. On that day, I knew immediately the Lord had me on an assignment. This had nothing to do with my nails. Rarely do I find that it's about me. If I forget, my husband is quick to lovingly remind me.

I knew the Lord called me to be a "light" for such a time as this. I never spent my appointment talking on my cell phone, texting or reading magazines. My focus was on the Lord's timing, what to say, when to say it, and how. Rarely did I mention Jesus; it was not the time. Instead, I displayed my life as a reflection of the love and favor of Jesus.

In general, we engaged in conversation about my life. Over the years, Ricky became quite curious about my lifestyle. He observed my love for people (we shared stories), my passion for fashion (noticing my choice of dress), the car I drove (learning it was debt-free) and that I went on numerous trips and luxury vacations over the years (fruit from consistently trusting Jesus).

Little by little, he became curious about my home, marriage and family. Every visit, his curiosity about my life grew. At one particular visit, Ricky asked me how I got all these lovely things. I casually replied, "It's Jesus." Jesus gave me all these beautiful things. In addition, I casually replied it's the favor of God on my life. I've learned that people respond to Jesus by what they see, not by what we preach. The conversation ended and no more was said.

Years passed by. One particular Christmas, I casually asked Ricky if he knew the story of Jesus to which he replied no. I never knew how difficult it was to explain immaculate conception to someone who had never heard the story of Jesus. I told him all about it and brought him a children's book with pictures about Christmas and explained the birth of Jesus on my next visit.

As the years passed, little by little at every visit, I gently revealed Jesus. One particular visit, seven years later as the incense was burning and Buddha was proudly displayed in front of me, I asked Ricky if he prayed to Buddha. He replied, "Oh yes." I told him that I prayed to Jesus too. Then I asked him if he talked to Buddha to which he replied, "Oh yes." I also said that I talked to Jesus too. I looked at him right in the eye and asked, "Ricky, does Buddha talk to you?" He replied, "Oh no," with a hearty laugh. I replied, saying, "Jesus talks to me." In return, he said, "Oh no" and I said, "Oh yes!"

I explained how he could have Jesus talk to him and shared how simple it was. He didn't have to earn it. I shared that it was a free gift from Jesus to him. I told him how much Jesus loved him. That same day, Ricky went home and surrendered his life to Jesus. He said to Jesus, "I want you to do for me what you did for Diana. If You're real, 'Come into my heart.'" It was that simple.

Today, Ricky is still on fire for Jesus. We're still friends and he's filled with undeniable joy. Anyone who knows him or comes into contact with him knows "his Jesus." At his nail salon when you sit at his station, you no longer see Buddha. Instead, you hear about Jesus, the redeemer of us all.

LIFE LESSON: You don't need to prove Jesus is alive or debate Jesus. You don't need to push Jesus, but you do need to patiently, lovingly and consistently let your light shine; Jesus will take care of the rest.

MY PRAYER: Thank You, Lord, that we have the freedom to show Your love. Please help us remember that although we may not always be preaching behind a pulpit, our lives are always preaching a message — the good news of Jesus. Amen.

HIS PROMISE:
"You are the light of the world. A city that is set on a hill cannot be hidden."
— Matthew 5:14

"Everyone who calls on the Name of the Lord will be saved."
— Romans 10:13

Hold On

"Do not become weary in well doing, for in due time, if you faint not, you will reap the harvest." — Galatians 6:9

> *We're required to believe God's Word, not fulfill His Word.*

If I hadn't decided to hold on when I wanted to give up, I can genuinely say that I don't know where I would be today. After failed marriages, struggling to find my identity, single and alone, it would've been an easy choice to give up. However, that wouldn't have been the life God intended me to have.

Instead, it would've been the life I would've *settled* for had I given up. Galatians 6:9 says, "Let us not become weary in doing good, for at the proper time we will reap a harvest if we do not give up." This has been the life Scripture that I've kept buried in my heart. During desperate times, I was committed to not give up.

My desperation to survive pushed me to dig deeper into a relationship with God. When I began to study, meditate and learn the Word of God, I realized that His Word would sustain me and keep me securely in place. His Word would support and bear the weight of any problem. I've found when He says it, He will perform it if we believe. We're required to believe God's Word, not fulfill His Word.

God speaks to us through His Word. When we read a passage in the Bible and it jumps out in our spirits, we can be confident that the Spirit of God is talking to us. It's then *our* responsibility to take His Word, put it in our hearts and hold on to that Word. Next, we're never to let go of what God has said until we see it manifest in our lives.

As a single parent, I went through some huge mountains. I held on tight to Proverbs 22:6, which says, "If you train a child in the way they should go, they will not depart from it." I would say, "Lord, You said, if I trained my child in the way he should go, he would not depart from Your path. Now, in this time of struggle,

I'm holding You to Your Word." If we hold God to His Word, He's faithful to perform it. He'll *never* let go of what He's said if we hold on to what He's promised.

However, we're responsible for the Word we're given when His Spirit speaks to us. It's *our* responsibility to hold on during difficult times and never let go. Whatever we go through in life — death, abuse, loss, poverty, divorce, bankruptcy, persecution, sickness — we have to be committed to holding on to what God has promised for our lives.

He said we'd be blessed and prosperous and that He would make rivers and fountains flow in the midst of our valleys. One Word from the Bible has enough power to sustain us for a lifetime. Our job is to hold on and don't let go. No matter what people say or do or what it may look like, we need to hold on and never let go.

If God said it, He *will* bring it to pass. Psalm 55:22 says, "Cast your cares on the Lord, and He will sustain you; He will never let the righteous be shaken." His Word has the power to sustain us and our circumstances, causing us to be stable in all our ways. We're only required to hold on to His promises.

To hold means "to keep fast, to grip or reserve, to bear, sustain or support." When the storms of life come like a flood, we're to hold tight to our grip on God's Word, which will support and sustain us through any storm. Refuse to let go of God's Word, even amid chaos and confusion. If I had let go of God's Word and not pressed in, I would've watched my destiny go out to sea.

When the devil says it'll never happen, hold on. When people say it'll never happen, hold on. When circumstances scream, it'll never happen, hold on. If we're willing to hold on and fight for the word God has spoken, God *will* be faithful to deliver our destiny right on time.

LIFE LESSON: There will be interruptions in life, but if we hold on tight and never let go, God is faithful to perform His Word.

MY PRAYER: Thank You, Lord, that You are faithful to Your Word. Today and every day, I *choose* to believe You no matter what it looks like around me. Help me to remember that if I bring to remembrance Your Word, You'll be faithful to perform it in my life. Today, I hold on to *all* Your promises You've spoken over my life. Amen.

HIS PROMISE:

"Hold fast the pattern of sound words, which you have heard of me, in faith and love which is in Christ Jesus." — 2 Timothy 1:13

"It's not that I've already reached the goal or have already completed the course. But I run to win that which Jesus Christ has already won for me." — Philippians 3:12

His Grace is Enough

"And he said unto me, My grace is sufficient for thee: for my strength is made perfect in weakness." — 2 Corinthians 12:9

> God's grace remains when we run away.

There have been times in my life when pain and hurt put me in positions where I felt like my life had been paralyzed. I often felt guilty that I had no words to pray, no words to say and nothing left to give. I felt depleted on the inside and felt guilty to provide or do something. Yet, I had nothing left to give.

That's when God showed me His grace is sufficient. After my sister died, I said, "Lord, You said Your Grace is sufficient, so I want you to know I love you, but that's all the prayer I have in me right now." Every day I would say, "I love you, Lord, but I have no words left to pray. I'm empty on the inside." Your Word says, "Your grace is sufficient when I'm weak." God knows how we feel and wants us to cast our cares on Him.

It's okay not to have all the answers and the right words to pray. God doesn't need eloquent words; He only needs an entrance to our hearts. He's protective of our hearts. Proverbs 4:23 says, "Above all else, guard your heart, for everything you do flows from it." When we allow God an entrance into our hearts, this gives His grace permission to sustain our hearts.

God's grace understands what we don't; His grace understands when we're not able. His grace comforts us when we're hurting. His grace brings strength when we're weak. Even when we run away, His grace remains. Indeed, His grace is sufficient in our times of need. Thank God for His grace in our lives.

LIFE LESSON: God's grace will do what we can't do on our own. When we're deficient, God's grace is sufficient. His grace truly is enough when life gets tough.

MY PRAYER: Thank You, Lord, for the grace to get through difficult days. Your grace is made perfect when we're weak and sufficient to meet all our needs. We can do all things through You who strengthens us. Amen.

HIS PROMISE:

"With confidence, let us draw near to the throne of grace, that we may receive mercy and find grace to help in time of need."— Hebrews 4:16

"God of all grace, who has called you to his eternal glory in Christ, will himself restore, confirm, strengthen, and establish you." — 1 Peter 5:10

God is Able

"Now unto him, that is able to do exceeding abundantly above all that we ask or think, according to the power that worketh in us." — Ephesians 3:20

> *Grace is God's holy ease to do what we can't.*

There is *nothing* God can't accomplish. God is able. Able means "having the necessary power, skill, resources, and qualifications." God has the power, He certainly has the resources, and He's most definitely qualified.

In addition, He's given us the ability to be partakers of His divine inheritance. Able is also defined as "qualified as having superior intelligence or knowledge." The devil wants to discount us; God wants to qualify us. God is able through His supernatural power and resources to get into our hands *everything* we need exactly when we need it. He *can* heal our bodies, our hearts and our lives.

He's able to get financial resources into our hands. He's able to bring to pass His promises. He's able to exceed our wildest expectations. More importantly, He's able to make all grace abound in our lives. Grace is God's holy ease to do what we can't.

Above all, God is so good. He wants us to come to a place where we *depend* on His ability to do the unimaginable through us. It's only when we know God's able that we're able to enjoy the abundant life He died to give us.

LIFE LESSON: When I can believe God's able, I'm able to enjoy life with the grace of His ability flowing through me, despite the circumstances surrounding me.

MY PRAYER: Thank You, Lord, that You're able to do all things in and through me if I can believe You're able to equip me for all things. Please help me to realize it's not me doing all things. It's only by Your grace. Amen.

HIS PROMISE:
"He is always thanking the Father. He has enabled you to share in the inheritance that belongs to his people, who live in the light."
— Colossians 1:12

"I can do all things through Christ who strengthens me." — Philippians 4:13

"And God is able to make all grace abound toward you; that you, always having all sufficiency in all things, may abound to every good work."
— 2 Corinthians 9:8

Preparation

"The preparation of the heart in man, and the answer of the tongue, is from the Lord." — Proverbs 16:21

> *We do our part, and God does His. We can't do God's part, but God won't do our part. Our role is to prepare.*

Over the years, I've learned that it's my job to prepare and it's the Lord's to deliver. In Proverbs 21:31, it says, "The horse is prepared for the day of battle, but the deliverance is of the Lord." This simply means we're to do all we know to prepare for what we're believing, and the Lord will do the rest. When I was believing God for a husband, my job was to prepare my heart for the one the Lord had prepared for me. My job wasn't to find him, but to prepare my heart for him.

Over the years, I've studied the Word regarding God's faithfulness, provision and deep love for me. If I filled my spirit with God's faithful provision and love for my life, I wasn't only believing but expecting my husband to show up and manifest in my life. By putting the Word in my heart, I waited with an *expectant* heart for God to deliver my husband into my life. We do our part, and God does His. We can't do God's part, but God won't do our part. Our role is to prepare.

The most important thing we can do is *prepare* our hearts. We have to know deep down that God's timing is always perfect. If the Lord had brought my husband to me before I was prepared in my heart, I wouldn't have been ready to receive him. We will not appreciate any gift we are not ready to receive.

I had to be at a point not only to receive love, but honestly believe I could trust someone to love me. My inability to trust would have destroyed the love the Lord had sent. We prepare our heart by first trusting God with our heart. It's only through receiving His Love that we're able to receive another's love.

Our affirmation has to first come from the Lord before we're able to receive or love another. Anything we believe for we must prepare before the Lord delivers. Preparation will set in motion God's timing on His deliverance.

When I believed God for my first home, I first bought the land. I could see the home I was believing for in my heart, but I prepared first by purchasing the land so I could build the home without having to compromise all the extras I wanted in my home.

It took me two years to pay off the land. Then the Lord delivered the perfect contractor and the finances needed for me to build the exact home that was in my heart. Preparation begins in our hearts. Getting in a hurry and wanting something now before the prepared and appointed time causes us to have less than God's best.

Two years earlier, I wasn't ready financially for the beautiful home, but I was preparing in advance for what I was believing God would bring to pass. Had I built a home prematurely, I would have had a home, but not the home I had dreamed of. I would have compromised to have it 'now.' If God has prepared in advance my destiny, I must prepare my heart to believe that He's faithful to deliver all He has prepared.

LIFE LESSON: I must be prepared if I want God to deliver what He has prepared. I can't do God's part, and God can't do my part. I must be prepared to do my part, and it must first begin in my heart.

MY PRAYER: Thank You, Lord, that I have the patience while you prepare my heart for my future. Help me not to be in a hurry regarding Your timing. I know the quicker I prepare my heart, the quicker You'll deliver. Amen.

HIS PROMISE:
"The horse is prepared for the day of battle, but deliverance and victory are of the Lord." — Proverbs 21:31

"Prepare your work outside, and make it fit for yourself in the field, and afterward, build your house." — Proverbs 24:27

Love Moves Mountains

"It is God who removes the mountains." — Job 9:5

> There's happiness after loss and loneliness.

There was a time in my life when I experienced so much loss that the devastation of my loss left me with no vision for my future. In one year, I experienced the loss of my marriage, sister, stepfather, grandmother, dog and my life as I knew it.

Prior to this, I had experienced the loss of my brother in a car wreck at age 29. My life was in total despair. It was almost more than I could bear. Now, as I look around, I see that I'm not alone. My devastation was preparation for a ministry of encouraging others along the way. There's happiness after loss and loneliness. Many people suffer loss; however, the key isn't to let our losses become our life-long sorrows. Loss is for a season; life is for eternity. I've learned to live with a heart to serve, as I live a quality and fruitful-producing life.

When we focus on our losses, it'll be the focus of our hearts. Proverbs 23:7 says, "For as he thinks in his heart, so is he." When we think loss, we become lost.

During this season of my life, God wanted me to be still. The devil's objective was to cause pressure to make me run. Therefore, I found myself running from my feelings, friends and the reality of my current circumstances. Although I was running, my life was in the exact same place as where I started.

Psalm 46:10 says, "Be still and know that I am God." It doesn't say be still and let Me teach you, be still and let Me change you, be still and let Me change your circumstances or be still and let Me heal your broken heart. It says, "Be still; know that I am God."

God wants us to know Him. He wants us to become intimately acquainted with Him during times when we are broken. God wants us to know His heart.

His heart demonstrates His character. God is kind, merciful, compassionate and full of grace. God's unmerited grace is sufficient in our time of need. He wants us to know and recognize *His* voice and become familiar with and understand *His* language, so when we hear a stranger's voice (the devil), we'll turn a deaf ear and flee.

He wants us to know He's for us and His thoughts are good toward us. He wants to prosper us, heal us and protect us. But most of all, He desires us to know that we can trust Him with our hearts. No matter who has hurt us, who has left us, who has abused us or who has spoken lies about us, God wants to make us whole. When I surrendered my Heart, God redeemed my life.

Today, God has restored my life, family and vision. I'm blessed, happy and prospering in every area of my life. I don't say this to brag about my life, but to boast about our God. The devil works overtime to produce mountains in our lives. However, when we know God, we know He's mighty to save and His love will remove every mountain that stands in our way.

LIFE LESSON: God is redeemer and His love moves mountains. The devil knows if we discover God's love, we'll recover our lives. No demon in hell can keep a mountain standing when God's love comes flooding in.

MY PRAYER: Thank You, Lord, that I trust you with my heart. Help me not to run when the devil applies pressure. I want to be still, so I can know Your voice intimately. I know my heart is safe with You. I know that when I surrender my heart, You will redeem my life. Amen.

HIS PROMISE:
"Be still, and know that I am God." — Psalm 46:10

"Though the mountains are shaken and the hills be removed, yet my unfailing love for you will not be shaken, nor my covenant of peace be removed," says the LORD, who has compassion on you." — Isaiah 54:10

Payday is Coming

"And I will restore to you the years that the locust hath eaten, the cankerworm, and the caterpillar, and the palmerworm, my great army which I sent among you." — Joel 2:25-26

> God will not only pay back everything the devil has stolen; He'll restore it better than it was before.

Everything the devil has stolen *must* be paid back in total and with interest. What the devil has stolen must be paid seven times more than what we had before. Payday is on the way when we grasp this principle of God. We can rejoice because payday is coming. Payday is when we're given payment and obtain what we're owed. It doesn't matter how far behind we are, where we live, what financial dilemma we're in or the condition of our health.

Payday *is* coming. God won't only pay back everything the devil has stolen; He'll restore it better than it was before. In 1988, my home was burned in a fire, losing everything I owned. I maintained a grateful heart because my children and I were unharmed. It's much easier to have a thankful heart when you understand that payday is on the way. None of the material things I owned amounted to much, but it was all I had.

The devil can't steal and keep what's not his to take. We have to decide not to live in the ashes, but move forward with excitement, knowing deep in our hearts that payday is coming.

As I look back and remember my home and the overwhelming loss, not only did the devil have to pay it back, the home God has given me today is 100-fold more than my previous home. Praise God for His faithfulness.

Twelve years after my home burned down, I suffered a betrayal in my previous marriage. Losing material things in a fire wasn't hard to replace, but the devastation of my marriage being over was more than I could bear.

As a result, I felt completely out of control. When we're treated unjustly, our flesh wants to get even. From a biblical perspective, the flesh is when our ways are contrary to the Spirit. Galatians 5:17 says, "For the flesh desires what is contrary to the Spirit, and the Spirit what is contrary to the flesh. The conflict with each other so that you are not to do whatever you want."

Finally, I realized that I had to let go of my justification and trust God for His vindication. Proverbs 6:31 tells us, "If the devil is caught, he must pay sevenfold, though it costs him all the wealth of his house."

Payday not only came, but it came bigger and better than I could have possibly imagined. I not only have a new beautiful home, but a faithful husband who honors his commitment to God and our marriage. God restores relationships, finances, careers, children and joy. God won't allow one thing in our lives to be lost if we *do not* give up on payday.

Joel 2:25 says it best — "I will restore to you the years that the swarming locust has eaten." When Satan has stolen years of our marriages, health, relationships and family, he *has* to pay.

If we quit living in our dead circumstances and start rejoicing in our living redeemer, God *will* restore better than the former.

LIFE LESSON: It pays to believe. We serve a God of love, justice and redemption. He'll not allow His children to be taken advantage of. He'll make sure we're paid in full all that the devil has stolen. If we can believe payday is coming, God will restore our lives better than before.

MY PRAYER: Thank You, Lord, that You are a God of justice and You will restore all the years the devil has stolen. There isn't one thing the devil has stolen that he can keep. Help me to remember that it's not up to me to get back what was stolen, but rejoice in You as my redeemer. Amen.

HIS PROMISE:

"Yet if he (the devil) is caught, he must pay sevenfold, though it costs him all the wealth of his house." — Proverbs 6:31

"For your shame, you shall have double; and for confusion, they shall rejoice in their portion: therefore in their land they shall possess the double: everlasting joy shall be unto them."— Isaiah 61:7

Show Up

"A man's gift makes room for him and brings him before great men."
— Proverbs 18:16

> On the other side
> of our obedience
> are God's
> blessings.

God doesn't require me to have all the answers to make things happen. He only requires me to show up. I've experienced times where I felt like I knew inside (Holy Spirit) to do something specific, but I had no idea where to start, how to orchestrate it or deliver the outcome.

I've since learned that my job is just to *show up*. On the other side of our obedience are God's blessings. God will move mountains and make room for our gifts. He'll cause favor to follow us and chase us down wherever we go. However, we need to do our job and show up. It's not our talent, but our dependency on God that moves mountains.

When I was a single parent in my 20s, I desperately needed money to support my baby. A job position was open for a fitness instructor for Richard Simmons, the exercise icon. I'd never been in the fitness field, but as a teen, I was a competitive gymnast. However, I could've quickly talked myself right out of going to the audition.

I had no idea what to expect or what would be required of the position. I also questioned if I was what this public figure fitness guru was looking for. After all, this was Richard Simmons. Surely he would want someone with years of experience to work for him. However, I was desperate for the sake of my child so I just showed up. Desperation isn't always the wrong position to be in. It'll cause us to press in, seek God and do what is necessary.

At the audition, there were at least 50 to 70 people auditioning in the first round of applicants. Much to my surprise, I was picked among the select few. I had no idea how or why; I just showed up.

If I hadn't shown up, I would have missed a pre-arranged

opportunity orchestrated by God. As a result of showing up, I pursued a fitness career for 10 years. I was recognized month after month for being the leading fitness club manager in production and top fitness instructor with colossal class attendance. My fitness center was recognized as one of the top producing facilities in the entire state. I showed up and God did the rest.

God will cause His favor to make us irresistible. Proverbs 18:16 tells us that a man's gift makes room for him and brings him before great men. No one can resist the influence of the Almighty. If I will do my best, God will do the rest. When we move toward God, He carries our problems away from us and crumbles our mountains. His Word says if He's for us, who can be against us. We'll never know the results of our obedience unless we show up.

I would have never met my husband had I not decided to show up. Most of the time, the answer to our heart's desires is God waiting on us to show up. I may not know what to expect when I get there, but I can always expect that God will be there, waiting.

God will make a way where there is no way, all because we had the courage to show up.

LIFE LESSON: If we show up, we can have front row seats to watch God do what only He can do. We don't need the answer; we only need to show up and trust the One who has all the answers.

MY PRAYER: Thank You, Lord, that You don't require me to figure everything out beforehand. Help me trust You completely and move forward in confidence that when I get to where You're leading me, You'll be waiting to show me what to do. Amen.

HIS PROMISE:
"Trust in the Lord with all your heart, and do not lean on your understanding. In all your ways, acknowledge him, and he will make straight your paths."
— Proverbs 3:5-6

"I will go before you and level the exalted places; I will break in pieces the doors of bronze and cut through the bars of iron." — Isaiah 45:2

God's Word Has Power

"For the word of God is alive and active. Sharper than any double-edged sword, it penetrates even to dividing soul and spirit, joints and marrow; it judges the thoughts and attitudes of the heart." — Hebrews 4:12

> *If I want a powerful abundant life, I must speak words filled with the power and abundance of His Word to back it up.*

When I began my walk with Jesus, I included Him in my everyday routine. I learned that the nursery rhyme — sticks and stones might break my bones, but words will never hurt me — was a big fat lie. Words not only have the power to hurt, but the power to destroy.

When I become overwhelmed with life, it's tempting to let idle and futile (ineffective and useless) words come rolling out of my mouth. Words can shape or break our lives.

God has been patiently teaching me that if I want a powerful abundant life, I must speak words filled with the power and abundance of His Word to back it up. He has lovingly shown me that I must first look to His Word to determine my life, not my circumstances. When I look at my situation square in the eye, it can appear grim and hopeless. However, when I look at God's promises square in the eye, everything looks different.

God's Word brings clarity. When we see through the eye of our circumstances, it'll cloud the vision of God. When I go through tough times, I stop and listen to the words rolling out of my mouth. I make sure my mouth is in agreement with God, not in agreement with what I see. We have to place God's promises in our hearts and speak them out of our mouths until the power of God's Word changes our circumstances.

When I believed God for my husband, I found Scriptures to back His promises to fulfill that in my life. Proverbs 18:22 says, "He who finds a wife finds a good thing and obtains favor from the Lord." I would say to God, "Help my husband to see me. You know where I am, Lord, so bring him to me." That word carried power. Literally, God brought my husband to me from Florida to within 10 miles of where I lived. God will do whatever it takes to change our lives through the power of His Word.

Any dead and hopeless situation can be brought to life if we put God's Word in our hearts, speak it out of our mouths and believe it until we see it manifested in our lives.

At one point, I heard the voice of the Lord in my spirit speak this Word, "Watch your mouth and I'll move your mountains." There's power in the words we speak.

LIFE LESSON: When I speak out of my mouth what I see with my eyes, I get exactly what I see. When I talk out of my mouth what God's Word says, I get exactly what God sees.

MY PRAYER: Thank You, Lord, that Your Word produces life. Any dead and hopeless situation can be brought to life if I believe Your Word, including sickness, finances, homes, marriages, children and careers. You're faithful to carry out the promises of Your Word. Amen.

HIS PROMISE:
"Then the Lord said to me, 'You have seen well, for I am ready to perform My word.'" — Jeremiah 1:12

"And God said, 'Good eyes! I'm sticking with you. I'll make every word I give you come true.'" — Jeremiah 1:12 MSG

"Jesus answered, 'It is written: Man shall not live on bread alone, but on every word that comes from the mouth of God.'" — Matthew 4:4

Stand Up for Your Life

*"And he said to me, "Son of man, stand on your feet,
and I will speak with you." — Ezekiel 2:1*

> *Once we decide we are ready to stand, it's an immediate victory.*

I remember the exact moment I decided to take a stand for my life by saying, "This is it. I'll not live like this anymore. I don't care how hard it is or how long it takes. I'll not waste one more minute living this way."

While in an abusive relationship, the conditions became increasingly worse each passing day. One particular evening, there was one final blow that made me take a stand. Then and there, I made up my mind *not* to give in and shrink back in my decision.

Hebrews 10:39 says it best — "But we are not of those who shrink back and are destroyed, but of those who have faith and preserve their souls." This wasn't an easy decision, but it was long overdue, as I wasn't living an easy life. Once we decide we're ready to stand, it's an immediate victory. To stand means "to rise to one's feet." The devil wants us to take a back seat; God wants us to rise to the front and stand immovable.

A few years ago, my husband and I visited a friend who decided to take a stand for their life. The devil had him trapped in misery and fear, as well as loss and pain. Through it all, he began to drink his life away.

He finally decided to take a stand for his life and admitted himself into rehabilitation. When we visited, there was a new hope, new courage and a new zeal to live. When we take a stand, God will give us clarity to see with a fresh vision to pursue. It provides us with the courage and strength we need to begin a new life. My husband and I left the center praising God for His faithfulness. The devil loses control when we decide to take a stand and give God complete control.

Joel 2:25 says, "I will repay you for the years the locusts have eaten — the great locust and the young locust, the other locusts and the locust swarm — my great army that I sent among you." God not only restores our lives, but He also pays us back. He's a God of multiplication who adds to our lives, making it better than before. It's best not to let the devil talk us into defeat. When we stand up, it's not over; it's just about to begin.

Dr. Jerry Savelle, an international minister, once said, "If you give the devil a ride in the back seat, before long, he will be driving the car." It may take some time to stand up and take our lives back. However, with Jesus by our side, He'll move our lives from behind and display us in front, with Him being the center of it all.

LIFE LESSON: It's up to me to stand. No one can stand for me. Once I stand up, Jesus will walk by my side every step of the way.

MY PRAYER: Thank You, Jesus, that today, I'll take a stand for my life. I won't let the devil keep me weak and defeated, as I sit and watch my life be wasted. As I stand today, I know You will redeem the time. Give me strength and courage to take a stand, so I can be a witness to others of Your faithfulness to give us a brand-new life. Amen.

HIS PROMISE:
"Who will rise for me against the evildoers? Or who will stand up for me against the workers of iniquity? Unless the Lord had been my help, my soul had almost dwelt in silence." — Psalm 94:16-17

"But rise, and stand on your feet: for I have appeared to you for this purpose, to make you a minister and a witness both of these things which you have seen, and of those things in the which I will appear to you." — Acts 26:16

Our Lives Follow Our Mouths

"From the same mouth come blessing and cursing.
My brothers, these things ought not to be so." — James 3:10

> Every time we speak negatively, it gives the devil strength and power over our lives.

A powerful truth I've learned is that our lives follow the direction of our mouths. One of the most excellent tools I contribute to experiencing the abundant life is being delivered from my mouth. This is a work that's continued in my life. Our mouths have the power to discourage, cause anxiety or destroy. God intended our mouths to encourage, speak comfort and produce life.

After being divorced for 10 years, I vividly remember how miserable I was. The more I fed my spirit with complaining and agreeing with the way I *felt*, the worse my life became. When I finally decided to speak God's truth over my life, my words began to change my life. I'd read God's Word and then repeat back to Him what I received.

Here are some examples:

1. Thank You, Lord, that I'm continually satisfied with good things such as Your love and mercy is forever (Psalm 103:5; 136:2), Your goodness and favor will chase me down (Psalm 23:6), You will never leave me or forsake me in my weakness (Deuteronomy 31:6) and Your strength is made perfect in my weakness (2 Corinthians 12:9).

2. In Your Word, it says that he who finds a wife is a good thing (Proverbs 18:22). I desire to be married. I know being married is a good thing, so I thank You in advance for bringing my husband to me. I know that Your Word says that You will give me the desires of my heart.

When we agree with what we see going on around our world, we become anxious, stressed and tense. When we agree with God's words and begin to speak them with our mouths, everything looks different, making our lives line up with the truth we're speaking.

We speak what we believe. When we speak words against God's Word, we feed our flesh. Our flesh is our will and emotions, reacting and doing what we want and saying what we want when we want to. The flesh craves what we want now. Satan wants us to continually feed our flesh with large appetizing meals so it can grow stronger and have a stronghold over our lives.

When we feed our spirits, the truth of Gods' living Word causes our spirits to grow stronger. It will provide spiritual strength to overcome any obstacle when all hell is breaking loose in our lives. To say it bluntly, our lives go in the direction of our mouths.

The devil wants to kill our dreams, destroy our lives and steal our destiny by getting us to speak defeat with our mouths. Every time we speak negatively, it gives the devil strength and power over our lives. However, when we feed our spirits, it gives our spirits the power and strength to endure.

It can become a bad habit to speak what we see, but it's a habit that can be broken by the grace of God. God's grace isn't to help us cope with life, but to live victorious lives.

If we get in the habit of agreeing with God's Word today, we'll see our lives begin to flourish. One day, we'll look back and see our lives followed the direction of our mouths.

LIFE LESSON: I must agree with God and not with what I see. I have the *choice* to speak harmful lies or the truth of God's Word. The words I speak determines the destination I desire to go.

MY PRAYER: Thank You, Lord, for giving me strength to trust You, and not allow myself to be overwhelmed with my mouth. Help me to use my mouth as a tool to edify and build up, not complain and tear down. I choose to honor You by refraining what comes out of my mouth. Amen.

HIS PROMISE:
"In the multitude of words there wanteth not sin: but he that refrains his lips is wise." — Proverbs 10:19

"So shall my word be that goes out from my mouth; it shall not return to me empty, but it shall accomplish that which I purpose, and shall succeed in the thing for which I sent it." — Isaiah 55:11

God Has the Answer

"Submit yourselves, therefore, to God.
Resist the devil, and he will flee from you." — James 4:7

> *It's hard to see the answer when we're buried in the problem.*

The power in resisting the devil is in submitting to God. Submission is not an act we do, but an attitude of the heart that we demonstrate. I spent many years rebuking (sternly pointing out error) the devil when I needed to be submitting to God.

Although my life was under attack and the devil had a plan, little did I know that my best defense was to submit to God. Too often, I got submission confused with concession. Submission is when you yield to the power or authority, where concession is when you acknowledge, as accurate, your opponent's victory.

When we give in and acknowledge the devil, that's a problem. When we submit to God, that's the answer. Our biggest problem is when we don't understand we're often the problem.

When my heart becomes hardened to life circumstances, I can't see the answer when it's standing in front of me. It's hard to see the answer when we're buried in the problem.

The devil knows that if he can keep the door to our hearts closed, it'll be difficult for us to see the answer walk in. My reaction in the past when the devil would attack was to close the door to my heart and distance myself from people. The enemy wants us standing alone and helpless, so we have no one standing with us at the battle line. What a trap!

In addition, the devil always perverts the truth. The truth is we're meant to be *set apart* from the world and devoted to God's purpose. When my heart was pliable and willing to yield to God, He was able to influence and mold me into His Image, as well as His way of doing things.

Satan wants to harden our hearts to God; God wants to harden our hearts to difficulties. When we become hardened to the devil's schemes, we know that although God has promised us that in this world, we will have tribulations, we can still be in a good state of mind because Jesus has *already* defeated the devil.

LIFE LESSON: To resist the devil, I must submit to God. A hardened heart has the doors closed and can't see when God is standing and is unable to hear when He calls.

MY PRAYER: Thank You, Lord, that You help me to submit to You in everything, so I'm in a position where the devil can't take anything. Help me to be quick to recognize the symptoms of a hardened heart. Amen.

HIS PROMISE:
"These things I have spoken unto you, that in me ye might have peace. In the world ye shall have tribulation: but be of good cheer; I have overcome the world." — John 16:33

"Fear not [there is nothing to fear], for I am with you; do not look around you in terror and be dismayed, for I am your God." — Isaiah 41:10

God Has a Way Out

"When you pass through the waters, I will be with you; And through the rivers, they shall not overflow you. When you walk through the fire, you shall not be burned, Nor shall the flame scorch you." — Isaiah 43:2

> *God's favor isn't based on our unfavorable conditions, but on His unconditional love.*

When adversity comes knocking at our door, God's Word always has a way out. There's not one thing we may go through as individuals, or a nation, that God's Word will not instruct us what to do. The Bible says that when adversity comes, we will not be moved, and our eyes will have the understanding to see the truth, and our ears will hear. We'll be able to see in our hearts and hear in our spirits what to do and when to move.

We'll be able to have confidence that God knows all things. Psalm 112:6-7 says, "Surely he shall not be moved forever: the righteous shall be in everlasting remembrance. He shall not be afraid of evil tidings: his heart is fixed, trusting in the LORD." When our hearts are fixed, it means we're fastened securely in our place.

I can recall a time where my entire life was in shambles. My marriage had been compromised. Then a few short months later, my younger sister unexpectedly went to be with the Lord. Eight weeks following my sister's funeral, my step dad had a massive heart attack. I was completely undone.

However, through it all, God kept my life secure. Secure is defined as "something fixed or fastened so it will not give way, or be lost." Although I became disoriented in my new surroundings, God never left me to find my way on my own. I was held securely in His arms.

In times of adversity, it's wisdom to run toward God before we run and turn the other way. Adversity is nothing more than something in our lives that presents an unfavorable condition.

Psalm 5:12 says, "Surely, LORD, you bless the righteous; you surround them with your favor as with a shield."

The good news is God's favor is for life. God's favor isn't based on our unfavorable conditions, but on His unconditional love. Satan uses adversity to cause weakness, so we'll not have the strength to fulfill God's purpose. However, God's Word gives us strength and is powerful and effective (Hebrews 4:12).

The Bible says a man of knowledge increases in strength. God's Word is God's wisdom that provides the answer to every adversity. It gives us a strategic plan to get out of every problem we encounter.

If we consent to adversity, our strength is small. Strength is not measured in good times; it's measured in adversity. When adversity comes, it's wisdom to not run from our problems, but run to our answers. God's Word has final authority and will override anything the devil throws our way.

LIFE LESSON: Adversity may make an entrance, but God's Word will make it exit. Greater is He that is in us than he that's in the world. When we are weak, God's Word in us will make us strong.

MY PRAYER: Thank You, Lord, that adversity can't have victory in our lives. In Your Word, You've given us the keys to fight any trouble. Please help us to feed on your Word so that we can fight strong. Thank You that when we feel weak, You make us strong. Amen.

HIS PROMISE:
"You, dear children, are from God and have overcome them because the one who is in you is greater than the one who is in the world." — 1John 4:4

"A wise man is strong; yes, a man of knowledge increases in strength." — Proverbs 24:5

Finding Strength

"The joy of the Lord is your strength." — Nehemiah 8:10

> *Love will find strength to resist and not respond to the devil's irritating deceptive devices.*

As I was reading the Bible, I came across a familiar Scripture — "You shall love your God with all your heart, with all your soul, and with all your strength (Luke 10:27)." The Lord impressed upon me how we take for granted the depth of His power and restoration wrapped into that verse. Isn't that really what we all want? To have someone love us with all their heart, mind, will, emotions and strength?

How many times are marriages broken because one partner couldn't find the strength to keep the commitment. I remember feeling so devalued when I found myself in that same situation in my former marriage. When we feel like we're not worth the effort to find the strength to fight for the commitment of our love, it deflates our worth.

During this time, the key word the Lord brought to my attention was *strength*. It seems that I often forget the importance of this commandment. Strength is defined as "the power of resisting a force, strain or wear." Satan is always roaming about wanting to cause strain on our lives.

Love will find the strength to resist and not respond to the devil's irritating deceptive devices. We need to find strength to love God enough to trust Him at His Word. He has gone before us to take care of our battles. If He is for us, nothing and no one can come against us and prevail.

It seems that many times it's the little day-to-day irritating annoyances that eventually evolve into the final blowout in our lives. It's like a leaky faucet, dripping continually into a bowl in the sink. Eventually, if it drips long enough, it will overflow.

God impressed to me that He wants me to love Him with all my strength. When I feel like people have mistreated me, I need to find the strength to treat them with love in return. When I want to have the last word in a disagreement, I need to dig deep and find the strength to love God enough to respond in love.

When I feel like my world is spinning too fast, I need to find the strength to slow down and spend quality time alone with Him. I know it took Jesus all the strength He had to be nailed to the cross and die for me, so the least I can do is dig deep in my heart, finding strength to live and walk in love for Him.

LIFE LESSON: I can say I'm committed to Jesus, but only when I find strength to truly live a life that reflects my love will I become a powerful witness. When I love Him with all my strength, He'll show me all His power.

MY PRAYER: Thank You, Lord, that You had the strength to die for me. Help me to find strength daily and live for You. I'm committed to Your love. Amen.

HIS PROMISE:
"And you shall love the Lord your God with all your heart, and with all your soul, and with all your mind, and with all your strength: this is the first commandment." — Mark 12:30

"So do not fear, for I am with you; do not be dismayed, for I am your God. I will strengthen you and help you; I will uphold you with my righteous right hand." — Isaiah 41:10

Age is Nothing

"Behold, you have made my days as a handbreadth,
and my age is as nothing before you." — Psalm 39:5

> *Our age doesn't*
> *define who we are;*
> *it defines how long*
> *we've lived.*

Our age is nothing before God. Young or old, it's never too late, too much or too long for God to get the job done. There are so many things that the world defines with age. However, our age doesn't define who we are; it defines how long we've lived.

Who says you can't own a beautiful home at 20 years of age or attend college at 70? Who says you can't start a business at 18 or 80? Joyce Meyer, a Christian author and speaker says, "Age is a number, getting old is a mindset."

Age is the life or existence of time we've existed, marked by certain stages or degrees of mental or physical development. We don't have to operate in our natural cognitive development because we have the mind of Christ.

Jesus will give us His wisdom at any age. We should be developing physically as the body of Christ by walking in His wisdom, which He so readily supplies. Age is a particular period when a person becomes naturally or conventionally qualified or disqualified.

God doesn't call the qualified; He qualifies the called. The world says you can't until you're this age or you must quit at this age. I'm thankful we don't have to live by the world's standards.

There's nothing God can't accomplish in us and through us, no matter what age. If God put it in our hearts, He will do His part. It's a heart issue, not an age issue.

Where our minds go, our heart follows. Once we get it in our hearts that our age has no relevance to what God can do, we've won the battle. The battle starts first in our minds. We have to begin each day by filling our minds with God's truth. The truth of God's Word will wash away the deception of the ways of the world.

Based on age status, the devil will try to get us to talk ourselves out of the lives God intended us to have. My husband wakes me up every morning and pulls me by my feet and says, "Here she comes a mighty woman of God. Demons are fleeing." As my feet touch the ground, he then says, "I love my virtuous wife." As I wrap my arms around his neck, we immediately begin to pray.

Every morning, I respond with a prayer similar to this — Thank You, Lord, for my husband and our marriage. Thank You that our youth is being renewed like an eagle (Psalms 103:5) and our age is nothing before You (Psalms 39:5). We have the mind of Christ (1 Corinthians 2:16), and the memory of the righteous, which is a blessing (Proverbs 10:7). Our eyes do not grow dim (Isaiah 32:3), and our ears do not become dull. We hear Your Voice (Isaiah 30:21). We will accomplish all You have set out for us to do on this day because our steps are ordained by You (Psalms 37:23).

When we program our minds that Jesus never looks at our age to get His Kingdom work accomplished and set our hearts to believe He's able to do all things through us, is when we'll know our age is no big deal to the God of the universe.

Be encouraged — Don't let age stop you from pursuing what God has put on the inside of you. Go for it. Your age is nothing before God.

LIFE LESSON: The longer I live, the more I learn that God can do anything, at any age, through anyone who believes that age is nothing to God. He *can* do all things, at all times and at any age to those who believe God is able.

MY PRAYER: Thank You, Lord, that there's nothing too complicated for You. My age doesn't qualify me; You do. Thank You for helping me to accomplish the things You have called me to do and that I continue to pursue my dreams despite how young or old I may be. You can accomplish all things through me. Amen.

HIS PROMISE:
"Then the Lord said, 'My Spirit shall not abide in man forever, for he is flesh: his days shall be 120 years.'" — Genesis 6:3

"He shall be to you a restorer of life." — Ruth 4:15

Stronger Than Excuses

*"In this world, you will have trouble. But take heart.
I have overcome the world."* — John 16:33

> *We have authority in the name of Jesus to keep our problems from overcoming us and becoming an excuse to live an unhappy life.*

I've made so many excuses in my life. Over the years, I've learned that any excuse I come up with to justify poor decisions or behavior is nothing more than giving myself a pardon to do what I should or shouldn't do again. Excuses not only become a reason to justify why we do what we do, but permission to continue. It's not what happens that makes us unhappy. It's our attitude how we handle what happens that has the final outcome. It's never too late to get a fresh attitude and begin again.

Where we start doesn't have to be where we stay, if it's not where Jesus intends us to finish our race. We must keep moving forward when disappointment comes and not allow our disappointments to be an excuse to live unhappily. When doors close, it can bring disappointment. However, most times in my life, God lead me into new doors by first closing old doors. One closed door is an opportunity for another door to open. What great news this is.

At 21, I was a struggling, single parent, throwing a newspaper route to make ends meet. I had to do whatever was needed to provide and take responsibility for the situation I was in. I learned quickly to find a way, not an excuse.

While we're hiding behind our problems, an excuse will overlook opportunities. All the while, God has provided our answer in front of the door we're hiding behind. God provides a way in and out, but we must be *responsible* to own our mistakes as well as take responsibility for our future.

We have authority in the name of Jesus to keep our problems

from overcoming us and becoming an excuse to live an unhappy life. First John 5:4 says, "For everyone born of God overcomes the world. This is the victory that has overcome the world, even our faith." We have the victory to overcome.

The devil will gladly excuse me from living the abundant life Jesus died to give me. Therefore, it's up to me to step in and not allow excuses to exclude me from living out my destiny in Christ. I've learned to be stronger than my excuses.

Three things have helped me to overcome excuses:
1. Conviction to my commitment is greater than the temptation to dismiss it.
2. I go to bed early and get a good night's rest.
3. I exercise daily and eat healthily.

We aren't exempt from a problem-free life, but we're exempt from our problems overcoming us and becoming an excuse to consume us. Romans 8:37 says, "Yet in all these, 'We are more than conquerors.'" So excuse me while I quit making excuses.

LIFE LESSON: Excuses will keep me from being free to live a quality life. I can continue to make excuses, or I can begin to enjoy my life and live it to the full.

MY PRAYER: Thank You, Lord, that You've pardoned my sins so that I can live a quality life. Help me not to make excuses. There's no excuse worthy to justify me not living the abundant life You died to give me. Amen.

HIS PROMISE:
"The thief comes only to steal and kill and destroy; I have come that they may have an abundant life and have it to the full." — John 10:10

"If I had not come and spoken to them, they would not have sin, but now they have no excuse for their sin." — John 15:22

God Has Our Backs

"For you shall not go out with haste, nor go by flight: for the LORD will go before you, and the God of Israel will be your rear guard." — Isaiah 57:12

> *We can be confident as we step forward; even if we make a mistake in our footing, God's at the rear to catch us when we fall.*

When I find myself in a place where I see disorder or lack of clarity in my mind between the right or wrong decision, I know that Satan isn't lagging far behind the scenes. The enemy wants us to retreat in confusion. Confusion is meant to make us do nothing in fear of something.

Joshua 1:9 says, "Have I not commanded you? Be strong and courageous. Do not be afraid; do not be discouraged, for the LORD your God will be with you wherever you go." Fear will retreat and go backward. God is with us wherever we go; we *can* go forward without fear.

I can't tell you how often I did nothing due to confusion. It's no threat to the devil if we never step forward. Every step forward we take pushes the devil backward. God's plan is for us to keep stepping ahead and leave the devil behind us. Once he's behind us, the Word in Isaiah 52:12 says, "The LORD will be our rear guard."

A rearguard is a "part of an army or military force detached from the main body to bring up and guard the rear against a surprise attack, especially in retreat." The enemy wants us to withdraw or shrink back from what lies ahead.

Hebrews 12:39 states, "But we do not belong to those who shrink back and are destroyed, but to those who have faith and are saved." If the devil can get us to retreat and discouraged from going forward, he can keep us from seeing what the Lord has waiting ahead for us.

In 1999, I can recall a year of total devastation, filled with an unexpected tragedy, loss and heartbreak. I wanted to go to bed and permanently bury my face under the covers. I thought happiness was in my past, with a bleak future ahead. However, God had other plans. He had plans to prosper me, not harm me, but give me a future filled with hope (Jeremiah 29:11).

Time after time, God has faithfully shown me that if I trust Him with each step I take forward, He'll bring up the rear for me, meaning God has my back. It may look like we're trapped with no way out, but God *always* has a way.

Even if we make a mistake in our footing, we can be confident as we step forward. God is at the rear to catch us when we fall. When God is watching our backs, our steps are secure.

LIFE LESSON: Confusion is a device of the enemy meant to hold us back. If the devil can keep our minds in an unclear state, he knows we'll not have a clear vision to step ahead into the life God has prepared. Be encouraged — God has your back.

MY PRAYER: Thank You, Lord, that You have my back. I know that when confusion comes, it's nothing more than a picture of the devil standing in front of me. Help me trust You with every step, knowing that if I make the wrong one, You're there to catch me and get me back on the path You've prepared especially for me. Amen.

HIS PROMISE:
"For God is not the author of confusion but peace." — 1 Corinthians 14:33

"For where envying and strife is, there is confusion and every evil work." — James 3:16

Strength for Today

"Finally, be strong in the Lord and his mighty power."— Ephesians 6:10

> *We have a role in putting on God's strength before we walk out naked and exposed before Satan, the god of this world.*

It's exhausting to meet all of life's demands. People and responsibilities can drain us of energy. While I was a single parent with a small child and working two jobs, I was barely able to meet the demands of each day. It was utterly exhausting both physically and mentally.

Unfortunately, demands don't lighten as we get older — they increase. This doesn't sound encouraging. However, God gives us the strength we need to overcome. Luke 12:4 tells us, "To whom much is given much will be required." Second Corinthians 12:19 says, "My grace is sufficient for you, for my power is made perfect in weakness."

God's grace is sufficient to meet every need we have, which includes strength for each demand life throws our way. Jesus taught that when we're weak, He is strong. He increases our power, which is good news. There's power in the Word of God to give us strength for each day. We can do all things through the power of His strength. It's not until we're depleted of self-efforts that we can release control and be strong in Him.

However, we have an action that's required. We must recognize that we're holding on, thinking we're in control. On the contrary, we need to release control. He can accomplish in a moment what would take the effort of a lifetime. To do this, we have to take off our old clothes (the old way of doing things) and allow Him to clothe us with His strength.

The Word instructs us in Isaiah 51:9 to put on strength, which is our part to play. Just as we have to take action in putting on clothes before we walk out naked before the world, we have a role in putting on God's strength before we walk out naked and exposed before Satan, the god of this world.

Strength is defined as "mental power, force, or vigor." It also means moral power, firmness and courage. To put on strength, we must firmly set our minds to rely on Jesus with every breath, every decision and responsibility He has entrusted to us. It takes courage to trust God for healing, our children, our hearts and provision.

However, the load is not ours to carry. I love what Jesus says in Mark 11:28-30 — "Come to me, all you who are weary and burdened, and I will give you rest. Take my yoke upon you and learn from me, for I am gentle and humble in heart, and you will find rest for your souls. For my yoke is easy, and my burden is light." Thank You, Jesus, for making provision and for strength.

The Lord promises to go before us and be our rear guard. The Bible goes into detail about the armor of God (Ephesians 6). However, there's no armor to cover our backsides. The reason is the Lord is watching our backs.

When we're busy protecting ourselves 24 hours a day, it causes exhaustion. It's not by our strength or effort, but by His Spirit, that gives us supernatural strength. God tells us to trust in His strength and not our own.

God divided the Red Sea and also covers us with the shadow of His hand and pleads our case. Isaiah 52:2 says, "Awake, arise, clothe yourself with strength, and shake off your dust. Free yourself from the chains around your neck." Another way to paraphrase this is leave behind the things that are weighing us down. If we continually carry the burden of yesterday, we'll never have the strength we need for each day.

LIFE LESSON: The decision to trust God at His Word and be led by His Spirit is the spiritual force that goes before us to give us strength and make our burdens light.

MY PRAYER: Thank You, Lord, that You're sufficient to meet all my needs. You've equipped me for today, and I'm strong in You and Your might. Please help me to remember the burdens of the world are not mine to carry. You're the Savior of the world and the strength I need for each new day. Amen.

HIS PROMISE:
"He gives strength to the weary and increases the power of the weak."
— Isaiah 40:29

"I can do everything through Him, who gives me strength."
— Philippians 4:13

Betrayal

*"But nothing covered up will not be revealed
and hidden that will not be known."* — Luke 12:2-3

> When we expose
> the devil, he has
> no power.

I have experienced many seasons of pain in my life, but I have found that even over death, betrayal has been the most profound pain I've ever experienced. Losing a sister at 35, a brother at 29 and both my parents and grandparents, I know the pain and loss of death.

Second Corinthians 5:8 states, "To be absent from the body is to be present with the Lord. Death on earth is final, but the outcome for the believers, Praise God, is eternal." This Scripture always gave me comfort in my soul and peace in my mind.

When my sister quite unexpectedly went home to be with the Lord at the age of 35, I wasn't prepared. Five months later, my (former) marriage spiraled into an unexpected outcome. My (then) husband took a job out of state and soon after was remarried. A surprise attack tends to make the impact harder.

The pain and betrayal of marriage, a sacred covenant, was more difficult than the death of my sister. It was almost more than I could even bear. What we don't understand brings pain. I knew my sister was in heaven, but where had my marriage gone? I've always been able to pull myself together, but this time I couldn't find myself to put myself back together.

As I was lost in all my pain, I once again tried to carry a burden that was never mine to carry. The pain caused me to close myself off and be out of reach from anyone who might've been able to pull me back up. I was all too familiar with the feelings residing deep in my heart — pain and loneliness.

Not just in marriage is betrayal painful to accept, but also in friendships, careers or any relationship where a bond of trust is established. I had a friend of 30 years who worked closely in our organization. At one point, it was revealed to me that there was a breach by my friend in our contract. I never dreamed it could've been possible. The betrayal of our friendship was harrowing to accept. Although she has aborted our friendship, I'm committed to this day to pray for her. What Satan means for harm; the Lord will turn around for good.

Unfortunately, in ministry and business, the people you think are for you are often the ones who ultimately try to destroy you. Betrayal catches you off guard. However, God is the master heart surgeon. Like a bullet in any victim with a wound left unattended, it can be fatal if not removed. A minor offense of the heart the size of a fragment, if left alone, can fester and create intense pain now and later, if not tended to immediately. The best way to resolve the pain is to remove it from the most vital organ necessary to live and thrive — our hearts.

On our own, we can't go deep enough to see clearly how to remove our inflictions. Therefore, it's easier to try and ignore the pain and pretend it never happened. However, when we least expect it, the pain will begin to fester and eventually cause resentment. Resentment causes our hearts to become calloused, pushing people and God away and making it difficult to hear the still small voice of God. This is the devil's plan from the onset of the betrayal.

When we smash our finger with a hammer, every part of the body responds. Both our hands let go of the hammer to grab our throbbing thumb, our body bends down to embrace our thumb or one foot may go up in the air as if to offset the pain as our face and eyes cringe to handle the pain. Our hurt thumb causes every body part to respond.

I have learned that pain is to be handled the same way. We're to let go and allow God and the body of Christ (the extension of Jesus on earth) to respond. However, it's difficult to respond to people hiding behind their pain.

Betrayal leaves question marks all around us. It plays the tape recorder in our minds repeatedly — play it forward, rewind it backward and replay and listen over and over. The enemy wants to torment our minds in ways that place blame, condemnation and shame. I was shamed into believing the betrayal would expose me as a failure.

Through this experience, I learned that when we expose the devil, he has no power. There's power over darkness in God's light. When light is shed on deception, we clearly see the problem at hand. God will send His people to love and support, not judge. The devil is the master of betrayal. If he can catch us off guard and cause us to be careless with the valuable things in our lives, then he can and will eventually succeed in betraying us and ultimately cause destruction.

It's up to us to guard our hearts against the devil by keeping God's Word in our heart as we embrace the people He sends during our times of pain. It is necessary to let go when it is time to move on. The enemy is lurking to see how he can expose us, be disloyal and unfaithful. But God is forever faithful, forever loyal and the restorer of the brokenhearted. I'm a living testimony that God restores broken hearts and makes life extraordinarily better than ever before.

LIFE LESSON: Behind every betrayal is the face of Satan. When we expose pain, we expose the devil. The devil's power is in darkness, but God's power is the Light of this world.

MY PRAYER: Thank You, Jesus, that You are faithful to put our lives back together when we have no idea how. Thank You for sending people to help us up when we're down. But most of all, I thank You for sending Your Son, Jesus. Amen.

HIS PROMISE:
"For all that is secret will eventually be brought into the open, and everything that is concealed will be brought to light and made known to all."
— Luke 8:17 (NLT)

"But everything exposed by the light becomes visible — and everything that is illuminated becomes a light." — Ephesians 5:13

Time is Valuable

"Be careful, then, how you live—not as unwise but as wise, making the most of every opportunity because the days are evil." — Ephesians 5:15-17

> Our *time should* reflect our *purpose.*

I can borrow money, borrow clothes and borrow a car, but I can't borrow time, which is a precious commodity. We all have the same 24 hours in a day, but what we do with our time will determine what Jesus does with our lives.

Time is defined as "a limited period or interval between two successive events." Our time on earth is just an interview between now and heaven. There's no time in heaven, only eternity.

Mark 13:32 says, "But about that day or hour no one knows, not even the angels in heaven, nor the Son, but only the Father. Be on guard! Be alert! You do not know when that time will come." Time used adequately can be profitable for life; however, time used poorly can be deplorable for eternity.

The Bible says there will be a time when we'll stand before Him and be judged (2 Corinthians 5:10). We will *not* be judged for how good we were, but by what we were called to do. Our time should reflect our purpose from God. What we spend the most time doing will eventually be what consumes us.

As for me, I want to be consumed with Jesus so that He will consume my life. It takes time to hear God's voice, learn His ways and build faith. It's worth our time because God is the redeemer of time. What I give to God, He gives back to me.

When I take time for Jesus, God honors my life to get things done more efficiently, more effectively and more successfully. The more time I spend with God, the more I realize there's no time to waste.

LIFE LESSON: Proper use of time has eternal value. I can choose to spend time doing things that will not profit my life or spend time with Jesus who will prosper my life. Jesus lived and died for me, so how I spend my time on earth shows what that means to me.

MY PRAYER: Thank You, Lord, that I have the honor to spend time with You. I choose to put You first and honor You with my time. In Your time, all things are made beautiful. I trust You with my time by giving You first place in my life. Amen.

HIS PROMISE:
"The time has come," he said. "The kingdom of God has come near."
— Mark 1:15

"Blessed is the one who reads aloud the words of this prophecy, and blessed are those who hear it and take to heart what is written in it because the time is near." — Revelation 1:3

Push Through

"Jesus said unto him, 'If thou canst believe,
all things are possible to him that believes.'" — Mark 9:23

> *If your dream has a 1 percent chance, God has you covered the other 99 percent.*

While attending a high school reunion, I talked with a friend about how I had seven grandchildren at the time. She went on to say she had none, but had a big surprise at the age of 40. She found out she was pregnant and was distraught.

She had used birth control with a 99 percent success rate. She casually said, "It may have had a 99 percent success rate, but my baby was 100 percent determined to be born."

Isn't that a perfect picture of when the devil tells you there's a 99 percent chance that you'll never have that relationship, never have that home, never have that career, never have that baby, never get out of debt, never be happy or never be healed. However, Jeremiah 1:12 says, "I am watching over my word to perform it." God is faithful to deliver. The devil has no way of stopping the sovereign hand of God when His plan is in motion. That's something to rejoice about. The devil has no power to abort the plans of God for our lives.

We need to be 100 percent determined to believe God at His Word and push until what we're believing to manifest is born.

Be encouraged — Your dream can not be stopped if God is pushing for you.

LIFE LESSON: We serve a God who delivers 100 percent of the time. With God, nothing is impossible. His Word is 100 percent accurate and is delivered 100 percent of the time.

MY PRAYER: Help me, Lord, to never doubt, but only believe You at Your Word. You're faithful to perform Your Word 100 percent of the time. Amen.

HIS PROMISE:
"With man, this is impossible, but with God, all things are possible."
— Matthew 19:26

"Rejoice in the Lord always: and again I say, Rejoice." — Philippians 4:4

Marked by Jesus

"You did not choose me, but I chose you and appointed you so that you might go and bear fruit that will last and so that whatever you ask in My Name, the Father will give you." — John 15:16

> The devil seeks to label our past in order to hold our future hostage.

It's been my pain and joys that have given birth to my words. It's the very thing that has challenged me that has changed me. It's the things that have pressed me that have proceeded my successes. It's the things that have tried to label me that allowed Jesus to set me free.

People love to put labels on our lives. They often label what they don't have or understand, which is nothing more than an opinion about who they think we are. However, their opinion has no validity because Jesus died to remove all stains, all pain and all labels. Yet, the world continues to try to mark us.

Jesus' opinion is all that matters because He took our place to die for our pain. When people are unhappy, they want to label others happiness. I've noticed that unhappy people tend to see through a glass half empty, instead of half full. They're stuck in their misery. When they're happy, they suddenly feel the need to label others unhappiness. The devil is the original label maker who seeks to label our past to hold our future hostage.

However, Jesus wants to mark us, set us free for His service and give us a future. Satan wants to place a label on our lives that would keep us bound from ever being who God called us to be. The devil tries to label us as losers, quitters, failures, unsuccessful, lonely, divorced, widowed, adulterers, barren, addicts, finished, etc. Jesus marked us redeemed, forgiven, beloved, conquerors, chosen and a finished work on the cross. Thank You, Jesus.

Over the years, I've found the very people who try to place labels are the ones the enemy has labeled. People who are opinionated most of the time don't have sufficient information to make a judgment call in the first place. Matthew 10:14 says, "And whosoever shall not receive you, nor hear your words, when you depart out of that house or city, shake off the dust of your feet." This can be translated — don't allow what others say or think hinder your thoughts. Shake it off and move on.

I've been blessed to be a successful businesswoman with a strong man of God as my husband and partner in our marketplace ministry, traveling the world internationally and sharing the gospel. We're all too familiar with labels. My success is because God alone gave me a talent, and I recognize that I have been marked by Jesus. It's not by *my* hand, but by *His* hand of favor. Frequently people want to look at the outside and form opinions about people who have experienced success. If they asked me, I would gladly tell them the reason for my success.

I attribute my success to trusting God through difficulty, giving at all times — even in barren seasons — hard work and pressing forward in the hard times. And most importantly — never quitting no matter what. My husband always says we never fail unless we quit. So now when people try to label me, I say, "You can't label me. I'm already marked by Jesus for His service."

LIFE LESSON: The devil wants to label our lives so others won't see Jesus has already marked us. The devil has no right to place labels. He lost all his rights at Calvary. Be encouraged — you've been marked by Jesus.

MY PRAYER: Thank You, Lord, that You have set me free. The world has no right to place labels on my life because You have marked me and set me apart. Thank You for choosing me. Amen.

HIS PROMISE:
"For you are a people holy to the Lord your God, and the Lord has chosen you to be a people for his treasured possession, out of all the peoples who are on the face of the earth."— Deuteronomy 14:2

"The world would love you as one of its own if you belonged to it, but you are no longer part of the world. I chose you to come out of the world."
— John 15:19

Live With Purpose

"Many plans are in a man's mind,
but it's the Lord's purpose for him that will stand." — Proverbs 19:21

> *There's a reason we were born. It's not to exist; it's to make a difference.*

When we're closest to God's purpose for our lives, the devil fights the hardest. The closer we get to our intended future with God, the more intentionally the devil tries to discourage us into quitting.

The good news is the devil is fighting a battle he has already lost. Psalm 37:23-24 says, "The Lord directs the steps of the godly. He delights in every detail of their lives. Though they stumble, they will never fall, for the Lord holds them by the hand." While Proverbs 16:9 says, "We can make our plans, but the Lord determines our steps." No man can change what the Lord has predestined for our lives.

In my early 20s, I felt the call of God on my life — a deep tug in my heart — and have always longed to do what God has destined for me. On many occasions, I've struggled with not doing enough, not doing it fast enough or not doing it at all.

Deep down, I think we all want to do what we were born to do. We want to fulfill our purpose and know we made a difference. It seems the more I press in — seek God and study His Word —, the more God reveals to me that I only need to do my best with every day He gives me, and leave the rest in His Hands.

His purpose for our lives has a determined end. We'll not miss out if our hearts are set out to please God. He loves us too much to let us miss our destiny. Before we were born, He knew us and destined our lives with purpose. There's a reason we were born — it's not to exist; it's to make a difference. We were born with purpose.

When I purpose in my heart to intentionally, please God every day by being sensitive that God is with me watching me and directing my steps, I find that every day I look back and realized that the steps of yesterday had purpose for today.

When I met my husband, the step I took yesterday placed my feet face-to-face with him today. It was a pre-destined step of my God-ordained marriage that I still treasure today.

I had no idea the day before I met my husband that my life would forever change. There was nothing significant or out of the ordinary I did that day when God arranged for me to step into my destiny. I just woke up, like any other typical day, with a heart to do all I could with the day God had given me.

Who knows, if you are single today, you may step face-to face with the mate you'll be spending the rest of your life with. God has a plan for everything about our lives. However, it's up to us to live each today with purpose. God has everything in our lives set in motion for each moment of every day and every breath we take.

LIFE LESSON: The key to walking with purpose is to purpose to do the best we're able to do with each day we're given. We never know what God has arranged to take place that day for those who trust in the Lord and do good while we're waiting.

MY PRAYER: Thank You, Lord, that today is significant. You have pre-destined this day. I'll do my best while I trust You with today, knowing that You have already taken care of tomorrow. I'm overjoyed to see what you have waiting for me today. Amen.

HIS PROMISE:
"The steps of a good man are ordered by the LORD: and he delights in his ways." — Psalm 37:23

"Trust in the LORD and do good; dwell in the land and enjoy safe pasture." — Psalm 37:3

Holding Grudges

"Do not seek revenge or bear a grudge against anyone among your people, but love your neighbor as yourself." — Leviticus 19:17

> *We have to let go of grudges so we can continue to grow.*

There are times I've been hurt and wronged and didn't want to forgive. Honestly, forgiving those who have wronged us is difficult. I've since learned that God called me to handle difficult situations. We have a choice to hold on or let go.

If we hold on to an ill will or bitter feeling, a seed of resentment will begin to form and start the process of a grudge. A grudge is defined as "when we give or permit with reluctance or submit to someone unwillingly." Grudges are caused by misunderstandings, jealousy, insecurity and pride, which leads to destruction.

Many marriages have grudges that have wedged love into a corner. Many business partnerships have grievances that have stunted the growth of the company. Many friendships have formed grudges that have ended friendships. The beginning of a grudge is the end of it all.

Grudges are a severe poison for future growth. Leviticus 19:18 says, "Do not seek revenge or bear a grudge against anyone among your people, but love your neighbor as yourself." Grudges will cause a seed to sprout that can grow into hate. The Bible says hate stirs up strife, and where there's strife, there's every evil work (James 3:16).

Most of all, grudges are dangerous. The devil is the master of deception, which is how many grievances begin. Simply meaning, the devil is in the middle of it all. If we want Jesus to be the center of our world, we have to let grudges go so we can continue to grow.

LIFE LESSON: It's better to let a grudge go, than allow a grudge to grow. A grudge today will stunt future growth tomorrow.

MY PRAYER: Lord, help me have a pure heart so I can see clearly for my future. Please help me to forgive those who've mistreated me and have allowed me to nurture a seed of bitterness. With Your help, I can let go of any grudges that I hold in order to grow and be all You called me to be. Amen.

HIS PROMISE:

"And when you stand and pray, forgive anything you may have against anyone so that your Father in heaven will forgive the wrongs you have done."
— Mark 11:25

"So if you are about to offer your gift to God at the altar and there you remember that your brother has something against you, leave your gift there in front of the altar, go at once and make peace with your brother, and then come back and offer your gift to God." — Matthew 5:23-24

Living Life Right Side Up

"And the Lord shall make thee the head, and not the tail, and thou shalt be above only, and thou shalt not be beneath; if that thou hearkens unto the commandments of the Lord thy God, which I command thee this day, to observe and to do them." — Deuteronomy 28:13

> God's authority causes peace, despite our circumstances.

Many years of my life were entirely upside down. At times, my life was going in every direction, but forward. Down is an English expression that means "things are being inverted or disordered." It means "to be turned so that the upper surface becomes the lower surface."

That's exactly what the devil wants for each of our lives. He wants the things God intended to be on top to be at the absolute bottom. Deuteronomy 28:13 says, "The Lord will make you the head, not the tail. If you pay attention to the commands of the Lord your God that I give you this day and carefully follow them, you will always be at the top, never at the bottom." That's always God's desire for our lives.

However, the devil perverts everything good that God desires for our lives to make us turn away from His directive. We're *never* intended to be on the bottom. I've had to fight hard not to let the devil steal my life. It was a fight worth the battle and a decision I made to have lasting peace.

The devil wants to take everything God has freely given to us and make us pay. He wants our lives to be filled with chaos and disorder. Yet, the opposite of chaos is peace. First Corinthians 14:33 states, "For God is not the author of confusion, but peace."

When my life became out of control and filled with chaos to the point I couldn't bear any more turmoil, I finally put my foot down and decided to stand firm on what God had promised — to bring peace and order to my life.

Order is defined as "an authoritative direction or mandate."

110

Therefore, it's a lack of order or a disturbance in the order. When there's a breach of the order, disorder ushers itself in without invitation. Satan's full-time job is to get us to go against God's sovereign authority to cause disturbance and disorder in our lives.

God's Word brings order, peace, balance and more importantly clarity. I've experienced painful years of my life where I lived beneath what God intended. Pain doesn't mean we have to live *under* our circumstances. God's authority causes peace *despite* our circumstances. Desperately, I tried to "dress up" on the outside so that no one would see the painful mess I was on the inside. God wants to come and address the pain on the inside of us so that everyone can see His love on the outside. God works from the inside out.

He brings peace on the inside to eliminate chaos on the outside. God's Word always brings order. His love brings comfort. If we allow God to do the work on the inside, the devil won't have access to throw us on our backsides.

LIFE LESSON: The devil wants God to be at the *bottom* of our priorities, so our lives will be upside down. Jesus works from the inside out to get our lives right side up.

MY PRAYER: Thank You, Lord, that You've made provision for me to live a life above my circumstances. I refuse to let Satan keep me on the bottom. You're the head of my life, and I will not live beneath what You died to freely give me.

HIS PROMISE:
"If then you have been raised with Christ, seek the things that are above, where Christ is, seated at the right hand of God. Set your minds on above things, not on things on earth." — Colossians 3:1

We Are Not Alone

"Never will I leave you; never will I forsake you." — Hebrews 13:5

> *Jesus will come in while we're secluded from the world and exclusively draw us in. He takes our seclusion and turns our abandonment into an exclusive relationship.*

While going through pain or disappointment in my life, I wanted to be left alone without anyone bothering me. The reality is I didn't want anybody close enough to see the sad state I was in. Although I was in a pitiful state, I didn't want to be seen that way. Therefore, I left myself in a position to not receive help.

Thank God that when we reject people, Jesus never forsakes us. By nature, when we feel vulnerable and wounded, we seek isolation. Thank the Lord Jesus that He never left me alone. He never quit pressing into loving me, and He never left me standing by myself.

To be alone means "separate and apart from others," but it also means "only and exclusively." Jesus will come in while we're secluded from the world and exclusively draw us in. He takes our seclusion and turns our abandonment into an exclusive relationship.

One of the loneliest and most devastating times in my life was when I unexpectedly lost my sister at the age of 35, and then a few months later found out my marriage had been compromised. A long-distance relationship my husband had formed with another woman threatened to destroy the core of my beliefs.

Thankfully, I was grounded in my faith. Colossians 2:6-7 tells us, "Just as you received Christ Jesus as Lord, continue to live your lives in Him, rooted and built up in Him, strengthened in the faith as you were taught, and overflowing with thankfulness."

If I hadn't been grounded in God's Word and his unconditional love, it could have caused me to be in a permanent state of rejection and insecurity. Although this was the most painful time in my life, it was also the most intimacy I've ever experienced with Jesus. My desperation to seek acceptance and love threw me into the loving arms of Jesus. I heard Brother Jerry Savelle, an evangelist and preacher, say, "If you are at the end of your rope, hang on." At the end of your rope isn't a bad place to be, since the only place to go or look is up.

What Satan meant for harm; Jesus will use for love. In my loneliest and most desperate time, Jesus made it evident that He was alive. When we press in during desperate and lonely times, Jesus will come in and fill our hearts with love and make an imprint on our hearts that can never be taken away.

LIFE LESSON: Although we may be in a place where we feel secluded, we're never alone. Jesus is alive and always by our side.

MY PRAYER: Thank You, Jesus, for your unconditional love. I know that You will never leave me. Help me to trust You when I feel alone and rejected. I know that You're always with me. Help me to be strong as I trust in Your provision. Amen.

HIS PROMISE:
"Be strong and of good courage, fear not, nor be afraid of them: for the LORD your God, he it is that does go with you; he will not fail you, nor forsake you."
— Deuteronomy 31:6

"When these things begin to take place, stand up and lift your heads because your redemption is drawing near." — Luke 21:28

You Can Do This

"I can do all things through Christ who strengthens me." — Philippians 4:13

> *There's no place you need to go that Jesus can't take you in a moment of time.*

Starting over is never easy. The reality of "it's over" forces you to "start over." Unfortunately, many people choose their lives to be over and quit living rather than starting over.

After a devastating divorce following my sister's death, I was standing face-to-face with starting over. It gripped my insides as if it had a death grip on my life. Jesus was continually saying, "You can do this." I felt I had an injustice. Everything in my life was going perfectly as planned, then Satan interrupted my life. I think we have all experienced *unwanted* interruptions.

It's challenging to have our lives interrupted. Life is going smoothly. Then out of the blue, trouble (Satan) enters and everything changes. An exciting truth that I've embraced is God is supernatural and can compress time.

In the Bible, the first miracle Jesus performed was turning water into wine at a wedding feast. He compressed the process of making wine into a moment. To be a good wine, it has a process of aging and maturing. The process of starting over doesn't have to be an extended period. However, for me, the most prolonged process was getting my mind to process it.

Romans 12:2 says, "Do not conform to the pattern of this world but be transformed by the renewing of your mind." Jesus can compress time and make our lives good now. We don't have to wait for a process to decide to move on. However, until we *choose* to move on, God will use the time to mature us in our spiritual walk.

Only when I faced reality and decided to move on, did my life move on. Often, there's a period that we determine is needed to go through guilt, shame or sorrow and for us to feel that adequate time has passed in order to move forward.

However, Jesus kept saying to me, "You can do this." There's no place you need to go that Jesus can't take you in a moment of time. He'll speed up the natural process, get you right back on His path and make it better than before.

Ten years after my divorce, I stood and believed God for my forever mate. Suddenly, when I met my husband, we were married 3 months later. God *supernaturally* sped up time, and we haven't stopped since.

In our first year of marriage, we accomplished and did more together than some people accomplish in 20 years of marriage. In one year, we traveled abroad in Europe to nine countries, sold a home, started a life together in our new home, had treasured time for my husband to know my mom before she went to be with the Lord, attended two Christian retreats and witnessed the birth of a grandchild. In addition, my husband came alongside me in business, forming a marketplace ministry. We also were both in leadership in our church for the men and women's ministries. In subsequent years, we haven't stopped.

God's plan is way bigger and better than we can imagine or dream of. God can do in one day what we can't accomplish in a lifetime. If we can believe through Jesus that "we can do this," Jesus will see to it — it is done. Be encouraged — You *can* do this.

LIFE LESSON: Life has interruptions, but that doesn't interrupt the plans of God for our lives. What would take us years to accomplish in the process of time, Jesus can perform in a moment and a twinkling of an eye.

MY PRAYER: Lord, help me to trust in Your timing. Thank You for strength to go forward. I know that in a moment of time, You can change everything. Help me to trust You, as I embrace each day with an expectant heart. Amen.

HIS PROMISE:

"In a moment, in the twinkling of an eye, at the last trumpet: for the trumpet shall sound, and the dead shall be raised incorruptible, and we shall be changed." — 1 Corinthians 15:52

"Then he told them, 'Now draw some out and take it to the master of the banquet.' They did so, and the master of the banquet tasted the water that had been turned into wine." — John 2:8-9

Everything is Subject to Change

"See, I am doing a new thing! Now it springs up; do you not perceive it?
I am making a way in the wilderness and streams in the wasteland."
— Isaiah 43:19

> *When I came into agreement with God, it didn't take long for Him to do in a moment what would take man a lifetime.*

Over the years, I've learned this fundamental truth — everything is subject to change. No matter who we are, where we've been or what we may or may not have done, things are subject to change.

Loneliness is subject to change. Sickness is subject to change. Being overweight is subject to change. Debt is subject to change. Divorce is subject to change. Being single is subject to change. Our lifestyles are subject to change.

Change forms our future course. It means things will be different than what they would be if things were left in their current state. Change transforms our current situation into something new. If I were left in my former condition when I experienced all of hell coming against my life through divorce, death, fear and desperation, I'd be living a life of misery today. However, I'm not.

Romans 4:17 says, God calls things that are not as though they already are. He called us whole in advance before we were even broken. It means that even though it's not that way now, it will be. What God called from the beginning of time to be will be.

There's nothing in this world that's permanent, which is such great news. However, God is an eternal God and His Word is forever. What we "see" is not what it is. God *sees* the beginning from the end in the exact same moment in time.

What we think is over is never over, unless God says it's over.

Matthew 19:26 says, "With man this is impossible, but with God all things are possible." We should never stop believing during impossible situations.

When I was a single parent, I was unable to pay bills, and was broken, lonely, fearful and hopeless. However, I knew this wasn't God's best, yet things remained unchanged. When I got to the point of where I was tired of feeling miserable and living pitifully, I made a *quality decision* to call the life forth that God called for me to have.

I began to call the things in my life that weren't as though they already were. I began to call myself debt-free, victorious, prosperous and happily married. When I came into agreement with God, it didn't take long for Him to do in a moment what would take man a lifetime.

God can do what we can't. God can do what medicine can't. God can open doors that no man can shut. God can afford what we're unable to afford. The only thing God can't afford is for us to get in agreement with the devil and say, "There's no way out."

There isn't anything in our lives that we get ourselves into that God can't turn around. I love what the Message Translation says in Zephaniah 3:9-20, "In the end, I will turn things around for the people." God has prepared a way out of a situation or circumstance before we ever got into it. Our steps are ordered of the Lord, and our destiny has been divinely planned. All things are subject to change.

Romans 12:2 says, "We are not to conform to this world but be transformed by renewing our mind." When we get to the point where we're *willing* to exchange our old way of thinking and let God do what only He can do, we'll see God transform our lives into something exciting and new.

LIFE LESSON: It's not over until God says it's over. Anything "dead," God can bring back to life. Every circumstance, every relationship and every life is subject to change. If we never give up, God will show up and change will take place.

MY PRAYER: Thank You, Lord, that though things may appear bleak, You have gone before me to prepare a way to victory. Help me trust You, as You do what only You can accomplish in my life. I believe change is on the way. Amen.

HIS PROMISE:
"I will go before thee and make the crooked places straight." — Isaiah 45:2

"I am God, and there is no other; I am God, and there is none like me. I make known the end from the beginning, from ancient times, things that are not yet done. I say, My purpose will stand." — Isaiah 46:9-10

DAILY DOSE with Diana

Suddenly it Happened

"I foretold the former things long ago, my mouth announced them, and I made them known; then suddenly I acted, and they came to pass." — Isaiah 48:3

> In order for God to make a change while we wait, we must actively be moving in the direction we're believing.

Throughout my life, I've learned it's wisdom to wait on the Lord's timing. When we wait on the Lord, our strength is renewed, and we will not grow weary while we wait.

However, waiting is active. I used to think waiting on the Lord meant doing nothing until He did something. When we're actively waiting, we expect Him to show up and show out. Hebrews 12:11 says, "Now faith is the substance of things hoped for, the evidence of things not seen." Faith is an action word and requires us to do our part. Our mouths must be saying what God's Word says about our situation, not what we see.

We shouldn't be moved by what we see, but by what we know is true. We know God is faithful, we know He's the source of everything we need and we know that with Him all things are possible to those who put their hope and trust in Him. When we expectantly put our hope and trust in the Lord while we're waiting, our *suddenly* will come to pass. Suddenly occurs without a transition from our previous state. God will supernaturally transition us from the position we're waiting for to where we could only be with His intervention.

In order for God to make a change while we wait, we must actively be moving in the direction we're believing. We must be taking steps of faith to demonstrate we believe God will make it happen. How can we believe God for a new home if our old house is entirely out of order and not ready for a move? What if the new home suddenly appears tomorrow?

How can we believe God for a promotion if we're not good

120

stewards of our current positions? How can we think our children's lives will be straightened out if we're continually complaining about what a mess their lives are? How can we believe we're healed if we're always murmuring about how sick we are?

We're to demonstrate with our actions and words we speak that we believe in our hearts that our suddenly is on the way. While God does all He has promised He will do, we're to do all we know to do. We're to stand and believe God at His Word. Isaiah 55:11 says, "So shall My word be that goes forth from My mouth; it shall not return to Me void, but it shall accomplish what I please, and it shall prosper in the thing for which I sent it."

When we put our earnest expectations and hope in God's faithfulness to deliver, we'll see our suddenly. *Suddenly*, our children will be saved, *suddenly* we will be married, *suddenly* we will be pregnant, *suddenly* we will be promoted, *suddenly* we will buy our new home, *suddenly* we will be debt free and *suddenly* we will be healed. When we continue to be active in our faith and get our mouth aligned with God's promises, our suddenly will arrive. It is then, that we will advance to the place God intended for us to be all along.

LIFE LESSON: If I'm believing for a suddenly to happen in my life, it is up to me to be actively speaking and walking with earnest expectation while I wait. If I am quick to see and believe it in my heart what I desire for my life, my suddenly *will* happen.

MY PRAYER: Thank You, Lord, that You are a God of the suddenly. Help me to believe and act on Your Word while I wait. I'm confident my breakthrough is suddenly going to appear. Amen.

HIS PROMISE:
"But those who hope in the LORD will renew their strength. They will soar on wings like eagles; they will run and not grow weary, they will walk and not be faint." — Isaiah 40:31

"Hezekiah rejoiced, and all the people, because of that which God had prepared for the people: for the thing was done suddenly." — 2 Chronicles 29:36

Change of Heart

"Moreover, I will give you a new heart and put a new spirit within you, and I will remove the heart of stone from your flesh and give you a heart of flesh."
— Ezekiel 36:26

We can't give away what we don't possess.

God seems to be more interested in changing my heart than my circumstances. Frustration arises when events cause our lives to go in a different direction than we intended.

God wants us to be able to hold fast to His Word and embrace His truth. His Word is the anchor to our souls. His Word will hold us in place when all chaos breaks loose. When our lives appear to be in absolute turmoil, His Word will keep us in perfect peace.

While going through a heartbreaking betrayal in my previous marriage, I desperately wanted God to change my circumstance and my husband's behavior. However, God was more concerned with the condition of my heart than my devastation.

Amid our greatest weaknesses, we're often tested. God will place us right in the center of our problem so we see it clearly. Then we have no choice but to come face-to-face with the situation at hand. It's for no other reason other than His deep love for us.

God tests us during trials for quality. He wants our character to keep us firmly in place as He prepares our hearts for where He's taking us. When we trust God even when things don't go as we've prayed for, He will make where He's taking us better than what we left behind.

The quality of our character will determine the quality of our lives. We can never move up to the higher life if we're afraid to climb to where the higher life resides. Higher means "of great vertical extent, such as the top of a mountain." When God takes us higher, it's greater than normal.

God doesn't have an ordinary, mundane, everyday life for us, but an exceedingly abundantly, above-our-expectations life. God wants to position our lives where we're situated *above* our circumstances, not beneath.

Under a dire circumstance, the devil will cause us to think that the way out is impossible, which is a big fat lie. We're not *under* the devil's thumb; *he* is under our feet. So many times, when my heart was crying out to the Lord that I wanted this, I needed that or I can't go on without this, God was revealing to me that my heart wasn't secure in Him. He wanted me to need Him and be all that mattered. When the time is right, God will not only give us what we desire, but what we need. If we get what we want at the wrong time, the blessing will be abused.

If the Lord had delivered my gift (my husband) before I was ready, I would've abused the gift of love God had placed in my life and ultimately lose it. My heart wasn't prepared to love, let alone be loved. We cannot give away what we do not possess.

When my heart was fragmented and wounded in 100 pieces, how could I possibly love with my whole heart? God knew He had to heal my heart so that I could receive love. If I couldn't receive His love, how could I receive another's love? It was totally a heart issue.

God had to put me face-to-face with His heart to reveal my heart. It was in seeing God's heart, that He revealed to me the condition of my heart. It was feeling His Love, that showed me what true love really is.

If I'm in a place where I feel like things aren't going well, I look deep inside my heart. When I get my heart right, suddenly my life becomes all right. A good heart produces a good life.

LIFE LESSON: God isn't interested in changing my circumstances until He changes the condition of my heart. If I want a life filled with all God has for me, I need to receive the fullness of all that God is.

MY PRAYER: Thank You, Lord, that You hear my prayers and will answer them when I'm ready to receive what You've prepared for me. Amen.

HIS PROMISE:
"Above all else, guard your heart, for everything you do flows from it."
— Proverbs 4:23

"Then it happened when he turned his back to leave Samuel, God changed his heart; and all those signs came about on that day." — 1 Samuel 10:9

Hope in Disappointment

"And hope does not disappoint us because God has poured out his love into our hearts by the Holy Spirit, whom he has given us." — Romans 5:5

> *Hope leaves our expectations feeling everything will turn out for the best.*

During painful experiences, I'd often feel like God disappointed me. There were events in my life I didn't understand; therefore, I would become disappointed with the outcomes.

The reality of my disappointment was faith to be delivered. The deliverer sets us free and releases us from bondage. My disappointment was my lack of trust in God. Inevitably, my disappointment failed to fulfill my expectations.

Our expectations must be in Jesus alone. The devil plans to cause frustration so that we'll give up on God. But God is the Father of hope. Proverbs 13:12 says, "Hope deferred makes the heart sick." Jesus wants to fill us with His love, joy and peace so that we'll overflow in His hope.

Jesus has a good plan for our lives with promising futures. He wants us to prosper in *every* area of our lives — mentally, emotionally, socially, physically and financially to where nothing is missing, and nothing is broken or out of order in our lives.

Hope leaves our expectations feeling everything will turn out for the best. Faith in God *never* disappoints. Hebrews 11:1 tells us that faith is the substance of what we hope for, and the earnest expectations of what we are hoping for will come to pass. When we put our expectations in people, money, possessions, etc., they'll always bring disappointment.

Through many experiences, I've learned that I can't think that my faith will override someone else's will. God gave us free will; that's the loving God we serve. He'll never override our decisions — that's why He gave us a *choice* to receive His salvation and love.

When my mom was in the hospital with terminal cancer, she lived out of state. I'd been waiting for her to get better before I came to visit so that she could enjoy my stay. However, she never got better, so my husband and I went to see her.

I was disappointed to see her in the hospital bed sick. I was disappointed to hear all the talk about sickness and death from family around her. I was disappointed that once again I was about to experience loss. But this time it was my mom of all people. Why?

Didn't God know that I already lost my brother at the age of 29 in a car wreck? Didn't He see my pain after losing my sister at the age of 35 to a kidney transplant? Didn't He understand the pain I felt when I lost my dad to chronic lung disease two years earlier?

In order to drown out the voice of God, the devil loves to scream in our ears, "Jesus does not care." Jesus sees our pain, and He cares. He knows all things and He knows and understands every aspect of our emotions, pain and disappointment.

Eventually, my mom did go home to be with the Lord. Many factors came about to reach that decision, but the decision was ultimately hers and not mine. It's not up to me to question God, but to trust Him even in my disappointment.

When I rely on God's strength, His ability, His integrity and His responsibility for my life *in my disappointment*, He is faithful to carry me through every disappointment.

LIFE LESSON: It's not up to me to understand disappointment, but it is up to me to have faith in God and trust Him with the disappointment. When our hope is in Jesus alone, in the end, we'll not be disappointed.

MY PRAYER: Thank You, Lord, that when disappointment comes, You are there by my side. Help me to trust in You with every detail of my life. You have shown me that there is nothing You will not do for me. Amen.

HIS PROMISE:

"May the God of hope fill you with all joy and peace in believing so that by the power of the Holy Spirit, you may abound in hope." — Romans 15:13

"Why, my soul, are you downcast? Why so disturbed within me? Put your hope in God, for I will yet praise him, my Savior, and my God." — Psalm 43:5

Self-Worth

"He saved us, not because of works done by us in righteousness, but according to his mercy, by the washing of regeneration and renewal of the Holy Spirit."
— Titus 3:5

We may have made mistakes in the past, but the price Jesus paid to give us life outweighs any mistake we may have made along the way.

For years, I struggled with self-worth. The image I had of my worth reflected the places I went, how I dressed and who I dated. My life was in perfect alignment with my heart. However, the reflection we see of ourselves in our hearts aligns with what others see in our lives.

In the past, I made mistakes that tried to define my self-worth. The Bible says we're to walk worthy of the Lord, fully pleasing Him, being fruitful in every good work and increasing in the knowledge of God (Colossians 1:10).

Worthy simple means "something of sufficient weight." Worth is a scale that measures our value, character and merit in our lives, justifying our commendable qualities. When something is worthy, it's of commendable excellence. Jesus is worthy.

The book of Psalms says, "How great is the Lord, how deserving He is of our Praise" (Psalm 145:3). His worth in our lives should have sufficient weight to support how worthy He is in our hearts. Our hearts reflect our lives and out of the abundance of our hearts flows the quality of our lives.

The quality of our lives should reflect our actions and words. Having experienced physical and verbal abuse in my past, I relate to those whose self-worth has been stripped. Jesus, and He alone, is the scale that weighs our worth. Our lives should reflect what Jesus has done on the cross for us, not by what we feel or don't feel.

How I feel about myself doesn't weigh my worth. First John

4:17 says, "As He is, so am I."

Jesus is worthy, so I'm worthy. If I allow my feelings to dictate my worth, my life will follow the direction of my feelings. Unworthy feelings reduce unworthy actions, which leads to an unworthy life. Shame and guilt lead our feelings to decrease our value and worthiness.

As a young single parent, I made wrong choices, which produced a shift in my life. Ultimately, this shift caused me to shift my perspective of God's direction for my life. The devil was screaming in my ear, "You made your bed, now lie in it." This meant that I had made decisions that got me where I was, so that's how it would be forever, which is a lie straight from the devil himself.

God *always* has the final say. He says, "We are worthy." He went ahead of us to pay the price so we could live lives worthy of the price He paid despite our shortcomings. Thank You, Jesus. We all have made mistakes, but the price Jesus paid to give us life outweighs any mistake we may have made along the way. I'm worthy of Him, so I should live a life worthy of all He has done for me.

LIFE LESSON: Jesus paid a high price for our lives. He is worthy, so my life should reflect the position and weight He holds in my life. My self-worth should reflect Jesus and His worth in my life.

MY PRAYER: Thank You, Lord, that You are worthy of my attention and love. Help me to live a life worthy of the price You paid. As I walk worthy of the call on my life, please remind me daily that my feelings have no weight on my self-worth. Amen.

HIS PROMISE:
"For great is the Lord and most worthy of praise; He is to be feared above all gods." — Psalm 96:4

"That you may walk worthy of the Lord, fully pleasing Him, being fruitful in every good work, and increasing in the knowledge of God, and strengthened in all might." — Colossians 1:10

Sleep

"A little sleep, a little slumber, a little folding of the hands to rest and poverty will come on you like a thief and scarcity like an armed man."
— Proverbs 24:33-34

> *When we don't understand our purpose, it will trouble us in the midnight hours as we toss and turn with uneasiness.*

For many years, I didn't get proper sleep. Some people never sleep, and some sleep too much. These are two illustrations of how the Lord never intended us to live. The Bible has much to say about these bipolar aspects of sleep. We're not to live to rest. However, we have to sleep to live productive and healthy lives.

Proverbs 20:13 says, "Love not to sleep, lest we come to poverty." Too much sleep is a road to disaster. God tells us He gives His beloved sleep. Sleep is a gift from God. When we don't understand the value of a gift, we abuse it to the extent that our bodies don't get the proper sleep.

There was a time in my life where I felt guilty about sleeping. I had so much I needed to accomplish before my day ended. In my eyes, if I didn't finish what I needed to accomplish, it didn't amount to a good day. My worth was based on my own accomplishments. When we don't understand our purpose, it will trouble us in the midnight hours as we toss and turn with uneasiness.

And it's during this midnight hour that the devil loves to taunt us. However, God is the deliverer in the midnight hour. Guilt of any kind will keep a person from sleeping. Guilt comes in all forms. False guilt is condemnation. Yet conviction guilt is from the Holy Spirit, tugging at our hearts when we're doing something we know we shouldn't. It can be as simple as walking with anger and resentment toward someone (innocent or not) or something bigger such as drug addiction, a marital affair or a false accusation.

When I was single for many years, I would be afraid that someone would break into my home, helpless without a man to defend me. Fear causes dread and what we dread, we avoid. In order to feel in control of my environment, I stayed up late every night, avoiding sleep. Yet, God has an excellent remedy for a good night's sleep. It's a matter of recognizing that we're abusing the gift of sleep, leading us to acknowledge to God that we need help and allowing Him to begin the process to getting us back on track.

When it's time for bed, my husband makes me laugh. The moment he lays down his head down on his pillow, he's out. I'll go to say something to him, and the heavy breathing of sleep is already in motion. How can you already be asleep? He jokingly says, "I have a clear conscience." Typically, I can fall asleep within five to 10 minutes, but one second? How is that possible?

All kinds of fears can cause a lack of sleep — fear of being alone, fear of the dark, fear of evil, fear of sickness, fear of death, fear of unpaid bills, fear of our children's safety, fear of tomorrow, etc. However, fear is of the devil. Fear is meant to cause us to worry and have anxiety. Worry *never* changes anything. If we continually meditate on God's Word throughout the day, God's Word will continue to minister to us throughout the night. Be encouraged — Your purpose in life requires a good night's sleep every night.

LIFE LESSON: To rise up to the lives we've been called to live, we must lay down and sleep when it's time for bed. Sleep is a precious gift from God.

MY PRAYER: Thank You, Lord, that You give me a time for rest. Help me to continue to trust You each day as You continue to accomplish Your purpose in me throughout the night. Amen.

HIS PROMISE:
"When thou liest down, thou shalt not be afraid: yea, thou shalt lie down, and thy sleep shall be sweet." — Proverbs 3:24

"It is vain for you to rise early, to sit up late, to eat the bread of sorrow, for He giveth his beloved sleep." — Psalm 127:2

Immediate Gratification

"Wait on the Lord. Be courageous, and he will strengthen your heart. Wait on the Lord." — Psalm 27:14

> *Typically, I've found what I feel I have to have now I don't really need or even want later.*

I've found myself in more dilemmas over immediate gratification. Like many people, I've settled into relationships on many occasions in the past for immediate gratification. Immediate means "to proceed without a lapse of time." There's a necessary process, which requires time. God wants a series of changes to take place in us before we proceed forward.

He wants us to have time to allow Him to take us through the process. He'll love us, teach us and instruct us for future successes *before* entering into something new. Too often, we want to go immediately to the next level *without* God preparing us for what's ahead. In my past, I would get out of one relationship and immediately want to pursue another. I never took the time to process what happened and allow God to heal and prepare my heart for my future.

Anytime I find myself needing immediate gratification, I can assume that the devil is lurking nearby to help accomplish my desire. Unfortunately, immediate gratification has no long-term benefits. Typically, I've found that what I *feel* I have to have now I don't really need or even want later. What I'm willing to compromise now, I'll usually lose later.

When I'm not ready to wait on God now, I find myself waiting on God later. Why is this? It's because I've moved *before* God's timing and inevitably ended right back at the place I started. Only this time, I've learned to wait and trust God with my next move.

Gratification means "a source of pleasure." God wants our source to be Him and Him alone. He wants our joy to come *from* Him and our pleasure to be *in* Him. When I finally reached the place in my life where I wasn't desperate for immediate gratification, God showed me a lasting satisfaction that can only come from Him.

Psalm 27:14 says, "Wait on the LORD: be of good courage, and He shall strengthen thine heart: wait, I say, wait on the LORD." This verse repeats twice the importance of waiting on the Lord. Once I learned it was wise to wait on God, it didn't take long. And oh how the wait was worth it.

LIFE LESSON: There's a time of process necessary for God to mold us, teach us and prepare us. When we're patient to receive in God's *perfect* time, we will find lasting gratification that lasts a lifetime.

MY PRAYER: Thank You, Lord, that now I don't rush the process. Please help me not to be impatient with Your timing. When You're involved in the process, it will be just what I need in every situation and exactly at the appointed time. Help me to wait on You. Amen.

HIS PROMISE:

"For the vision is yet for an appointed time; but in the end, it will speak, and it will not lie. Though it tarries, waits for it; because it will surely come, it will not linger." — Habakkuk 2:3

"Be still in the presence of the LORD, and wait patiently for him to act. Don't worry about evil people who prosper or fret about their wicked schemes." — Psalm 37:7 (NLT)

Fight for Peace

"Finally, brethren, farewell. Become complete. Be of good comfort, be of one mind, live in peace, and the God of love and peace will be with you."
— 2 Corinthians 13:11

> *Peace requires transformation within before it can be manifested outwardly in our relationships.*

For many years of my life, peace was something that I lacked. Fear, abuse and tragedy caused my emotions to always be on edge. Through my desperation, I learned to have peace and that it was a *gift* that Jesus left for me to possess. John 14:27 says, "Peace I leave with you; my peace I give you. I do not give to you as the world gives. Do not let your hearts be troubled, and do not be afraid."

Not only did Jesus *give* us peace, but He also assured us that it was a gift that came with protection, having no need to ever be afraid. Daily, I pray that my family lives in peace with one another, perfectly joined together, with no division and encouraging one another with one heart and one mind. The pressure of this world has turned families against each another and caused much division in our world. Quite often, my husband says that we must fight for peace.

Hebrew 12:14 says, "Pursue peace with all people, and holiness, without which no one will see the Lord." The Message Translation says, "Work at getting along with each other and with God. Otherwise, you'll never get so much as a glimpse of God." Peace is worth fighting for if it's the very thing that will put us in God's presence.

Peace isn't something we can demand from other people. As a child of God, we have to walk in peace. It's a free gift, but we have the responsibility to receive it, and take it with us wherever we go.

In addition, we must guard what we listen to and watch, who we allow to make deposits into our hearts and what comes out of our mouths. What we say can stir up strife or provide a blanket of peace and comfort to those we're in relationship with.

The Message Translation of 2 Corinthians 13:11 says, "Be cheerful. Keep things in good repair. Keep your spirits up. Think in harmony. Be agreeable. Do all that, and the God of love and peace will be with you for sure. This is the antidote for peace."

This Scripture makes it clear that we're responsible for keeping things in good repair. Repair means "to renew or restore to a good or sound condition after the damage has taken place." Having experienced the sting of loss and betrayal, I understand the damage it causes in your mind and emotions.

Therefore, it's up to us to renew our minds with the Word of God and be transformed. Peace requires transformation *within* before it can be manifested *outwardly* in our relationships. We have to be still and let God quiet our souls. Philippians 4:7 says, "And the peace of God, which surpasses all understanding, will guard your hearts and minds through Christ Jesus." We have to *guard* our hearts to have peace.

We're not only to live peaceably with our spouses and those we're in close relationship with, but also to think in harmony with them. Our thoughts should be thoughts that support one another as well as affirm and encourage one another.

We can say one thing with our mouths, but if we're thinking thoughts that oppose the words we speak, we can't possibly be in unity. This is double mindedness, which causes us to be divided against ourselves. A house divided will fall. A mind divided against itself will emotionally crumble. James 1:8 says, "A double minded man is unstable in all his ways." Therefore, we have to live peaceably with ourselves. Who would've ever thought we'd have to get along with ourselves before we can get along with others?

The Bible says as a man thinks in his heart, so is he (Proverbs 23:7). When our thoughts oppose our hearts, we're not in harmony with ourselves. Likewise, when our thoughts contradict God's Word, we're not in a relationship with God, which is a truth that's hard to face.

It truly doesn't matter if our mouths are saying the right thing while our hearts deny the very thing we're saying. When we think in harmony, then we will be agreeable. The Bible says, "Become complete, be of one mind, live in peace, and the God of love and peace will be with you" (2 Corinthians 13:11 KJV).

God wants us to be undivided, uncompromised, entire, lacking nothing, having all that's required in our character and skill to be perfectly joined together in the image of Jesus. In addition, God wants us to be together in unity with Him and in harmony with each other. He wants to destroy the middle wall of separation and hostility that's running rampant in the world. If we're against each other, Satan's most significant work is done with little effort.

If we want peace with others, we must first pursue peace in our own hearts and minds. Where our hearts and thoughts go, our lives will follow.

LIFE LESSON: To be perfectly joined together with no division, we must learn that peace first begins within our hearts before it can be manifested in our lives.

MY PRAYER: Thank You, Lord. You are the Prince of Peace. Help me to live in peace with those I'm in relationship with. Search my thoughts and allow my thoughts to agree with Your thoughts. Amen.

HIS PROMISE:
"*I appeal to you, brothers, by the name of our Lord Jesus Christ, that all of you agree and that there be no divisions among you, but that you be united in the same mind and the same judgment.*" — 1 Corinthians 1:10-11

"*Now may the Lord of peace Himself give you peace at all times and in every way.*" — 2 Thessalonians 3:16

Leave it in the Past

"Do not call to mind the former things, or ponder things of the past."
— Isaiah 43:18

> *It's a choice to allow or halt the past from dictating our future.*

Over the years, I'd repeatedly drag my past into my present. After failing in relationship after relationship, I got in the habit of bringing everything from one relationship into the next, which is the perfect recipe for failure.

When we experience the sting of pain, it isn't easy to forget. I've learned you don't forget the *memory* of your past, but you *decide* to leave the memory of your past behind. Choosing to hang on to the pain of our past has the power to block the vision of our future.

It's human nature to hang on to our painful memories to self-protect our hearts. When we feel familiar pain, we immediately remember the pain and go back in time, responding in a similar way as we did when we first experienced it. Unfortunately, at that point, we start going backward. Jesus wants us to move *forward*. He wants us to give Him the pain and leave it with him.

Isaiah 43:18 states, "Remember not the former things, nor consider the things of old. Behold, I am doing a new thing; now it springs forth, do you not perceive it? I will make a way in the wilderness and rivers in the desert." God never intended us to drag our past into our new relationships. If we allow Him, He will make a new way and do a new thing in our lives.

Jesus will take the things that the devil meant to destroy us with to prepare us for a beautiful future with a heart filled with one precious memory — He died so we could live. It's a *choice* to allow or halt the past from dictating our future.

Jesus took the pain of yesterday so we could glorify Him today. Daily, I have to make a conscious decision not to allow what has happened to me in the past affect what God has prepared for me

137

now and in the future. I'm so grateful Jesus took my past to redefine my future.

LIFE LESSON: Anything in our past that keeps us from moving forward, we must choose to leave behind. It's up to us to settle it in our minds and decide to be done with it. If we hang on to our past forever, our past will forever hang on to us.

MY PRAYER: Thank You, Lord, that today is a new day. Help me, Lord, to remember that I shouldn't hang on to my past, or it will block my vision of my future. Today, I choose to move forward and leave the memory of the past behind me. Amen.

HIS PROMISE:
"Brethren, I do not regard myself as having laid hold of it yet; but one thing I do: forgetting what lies behind and reaching forward to what lies ahead, I press on toward the goal for the prize of the upward call of God in Christ Jesus."
— Philippians 3:13

God's Perfect Mate

"The LORD God said, 'It is not good for the man to be alone. I will make a helper suitable for him.'" — Genesis 2:18

> God knows how to deliver the mate ideally suited for each of us.

Several years back, my husband and I started praying for a few single friends at 4:00 a.m. When God brings us a godly mate who's a gift from God, we want others to experience it as well. When we pray, we call out each person by name. The list keeps growing and growing.

We never forget to pray for the single friends God has put on our hearts. It's interesting how we can recall each name, no matter how long the list gets, because we faithfully intercede daily. It reminds me of Isaiah 49:16, which says, "See, I have engraved you on the palms of my hands; your walls are ever before me." Jesus is at the right hand of our Father, interceding for us daily. We're engraved on the heart of our Father. What a blessing.

When certain people are continually on our minds, it's difficult to forget their situations. It's so exciting when our single friends call to say they're now in a meaningful relationship or getting married. Typically, our friends will express an interest in finding their soul mate, and we'll let them know that we'll faithfully be praying for them.

Last year, the Lord put one of my husband's friends on our hearts who has been single his entire life. Although he would never express it, he has always desired to find his suitable companion. This man is a good man; however, he most likely doesn't know how to apply God's Word to aggressively believe for a mate. We never told him we were praying. We hadn't even talked to him in over a year.

A few short months after the Lord put it on our hearts to begin praying for him, we were going to spend some time in Florida. My husband reached out to let him know we were coming to town. Out of the clear blue, he asked if we could go to dinner to meet his new girlfriend.

At dinner, I asked his girlfriend how they got together, as we've known this man for years and knew he had not been in any relationship before. She proceeded to tell us she had been married 25 years and her husband, at 42 years of age, died of Lou Gehrig's disease, which devastated her.

She lived in Mississippi and had not worked her entire marriage, except when she was 20 years old and worked in Florida. One day, the man she worked for 20 years ago popped into her head. She said, "I had no idea why he came to my mind."

As a result, she decided to go to Florida for a mini vacation. After all these years, something on the inside gave her the courage to write him a short note to let him know she was coming to town. They agreed to meet, and what a divine set up it was.

I can't express enough how perfect a match this is; they couldn't be more perfect for each other. It's truly a match made in heaven. Less than six months after dating, she moved to Florida, and wedding bells most certainly appear to be in their future.

When we shared our story about him being on our prayer list, it built up their faith and encouraged them of God's deep love for them. In addition, it was a reminder to us of God's faithfulness to His children who are willing to intercede on behalf of those He loves.

God knows how to deliver the mate ideally suited for each one of us. It doesn't matter if they're on the other side of the world, God will beautifully orchestrate a meeting. If we desire a mate, God will not deny our hearts.

In my case, I wrote a petition to the Lord for my husband (Philippians 4:6) and thanked God for him daily before I ever met him. After 10 years of being single, I met my husband and 90 days later we were married. We're by no means perfect, but we're perfectly suited for each other.

LIFE LESSON: God is good and will not withhold any good thing from us. When God took the rib from Adam and created woman, the Bible says He brought her to the man. When we join our faith with Him and believe, God will send us the perfect mate.

MY PRAYER: Thank You, Lord, that You have prepared the perfect mate to be a suitable companion for each of us. You said it was a good thing to find a mate, so I'm thanking You in advance. Help me to be patient while I wait on You. Amen.

HIS PROMISE:
"Then the LORD God made a woman from the rib he had taken out of the man, and he brought her to the man." — Genesis 2:22

"He who finds a wife finds a good thing and obtains favor from the Lord." — Proverbs 18:22

Focus on His Goodness

*"Surely goodness and mercy shall follow me all the days of my life,
and I will dwell in the house of the Lord forever."* — Psalm 23:6

> *If I choose to focus on dead things such as the past, it doesn't change the history or circumstances. Ultimately, it's a dead-end road.*

When I think about all that Jesus has done in my life, I can't help but be grateful. Despite the hardships and disappointments, Jesus has always been the answer. God wants us to focus on His goodness; the devil wants us to focus on our disappointments.

Regret brings sorrow and dismay; Jesus brings hope and encouragement. The Bible refers to regret as a way for Satan to get inside us mentally. Regret makes us wish things were a different way. Ecclesiastes 7:10 tells us, "Do not say, 'Why were the old days better than these?' For it is not wise to ask such questions."

If I choose to focus on dead things such as the past, it doesn't change the history or circumstances. Ultimately, it's a dead-end road. However, when I focus on all God has done for me, I see a victorious life. Even though I've experienced verbal, physical and sexual abuse, I don't spend my time regretting and tormenting the time I spent in those terrible circumstances. Instead, I thank God He delivered me out of the relationships and placed my feet on solid ground.

We have to think on His goodness intentionally. Philippians 4:8 says, "Fix your thoughts on what is true, and honorable, and right, and pure, and lovely, and admirable. Think about things that are excellent and worthy of praise." We must think good thoughts and focus on God's goodness on purpose. Joyce Meyer, a Christian author, says, "Do not allow your mind to be a garbage can." We need to focus on God's goodness.

When I remember all the times He's protected me by not giving me what I wanted, I can't help but praise Him and rejoice amid my problems. I've been reminded of the times He spared my life and gave me grace when I deserved judgment and when He held doors wide open that the devil tried to shut and gave His unconditional love when no one was available. In these moments, I don't praise Him because I have problems, I praise Him because Jesus, in all His goodness, is the answer to them all.

LIFE LESSON: When problems arise, so does Jesus. Jesus *is* the only answer to anything pertaining to life.

MY PRAYER: Thank You, Lord, that You are good and loving and have provided all the answers for me to have a good life. Thank You for all You have done for me. Help me to focus on Your goodness. Amen.

HIS PROMISE:
"According to His divine power He has given us all things that pertain to life and godliness, through the knowledge of Him that has called us to glory and virtue." — 2 Peter 1:3

"Arise, shine, for your light, has come, and the glory of the LORD rises upon you." — Isaiah 60:1

Trouble Your Trouble

"Submit yourselves to God. Resist the devil, and he will flee from you."
— James 4:7

> *When the devil brings trouble, it's not up for debate. We don't even need to acknowledge him or give him any thought or credit.*

We live in a fallen world. However, Jesus gave us a heads up of how bleak the world would appear. In John 16:33, He said, "I have told you these things, so that in me you may have peace. In this world, you will have trouble. But take heart! I have overcome the world."

In this powerful verse, He let us know that we *would* encounter tribulation, but told us not to be sad or concerned with our problems because He's already won the battle. When we have a problem, it's our responsibility to resist the devil, not assist him.

Assist means "to aide to a cause." It's also associated with an assistant or helper. When we don't resist the devil right away, we become his helper. One day I heard a preacher say, that when a problem comes, "Trouble your trouble."

When we complain, we're associating with the devil's ways and assisting him with making our problem bigger. When issues arise and we begin to complain about our problem at hand, we agree with what the devil is saying — "You knew this was going to happen. This always happens and there's no way out. Looks like you're in for a hard road ahead."

When the devil brings trouble, it's not up for debate. We don't even need to acknowledge him or give him any thought or credit. When we *praise* God, we're resisting Satan. Praise is a mighty spiritual weapon. Psalm 8:2 NIV says, "Through the praise of children and infants you have established a stronghold against your enemies, to silence the foe and the avenger."

Not only can we stop the enemy in his tracks with praise, it also has the power to silence him as well. When we complain during trials, we become weak. When we praise God amid tribulation, we gain strength, and Satan becomes weak.

The devil not only loses power, but he also loses control. We have to take trouble and assist God with our agreement, not debate. When I began studying the Word, the first thing I learned was to agree with God. We need to agree that He's God and is greater than any mountain in our lives.

In 2000, I faced a big mountain that I thought would crush me. After marrying a pastor's son, I never dreamed one day I would be face-to-face with divorce. The betrayal was more than I *thought* I could bear.

However, I had a *choice*. I could either complain about the situation or I could choose to agree with God that He would work out all things for my good. It was a challenging time and not easy, but God was and is always faithful.

God not only worked everything out for my good, but He also made it better. Although we divorced, God brought an amazing man of God into my life, and now we're in full-time ministry together. God restored 100-fold what it was previously. There's no other like our God. His Word has final authority. He's greater. He's the answer in all things, at all times and in every situation.

When I thought I would collapse under the pressure, I would say, "Greater is He in me than who's in the world," which is praise. I wasn't saying what the devil was doing, but only saying what God has already done, which gives Him the glory.

Our praise causes our situations to supernaturally do an about face. When we give praise to God, it honors His ability and causes us to take a sudden change in position. As we praise, we get aligned with God's purpose for our lives. We resist the devil by turning in the opposite direction and adjusting our stance.

When we resist the devil and turn our backs to him, not only does he flee but we suddenly find ourselves standing face-to-face with God, which is something to praise Him about.

LIFE LESSON: When trouble comes, we have a choice. We can either agree with our problem or we can praise God that He's the answer to our problem. The quicker we turn our backs on the devil, the faster we'll see the face of God.

MY PRAYER: Thank You, Lord, that in the face of trouble, You are there ready to fight my battles. Today, I choose to turn my back on the devil and stand face-to-face with You. I thank You in advance for my victory. Amen.

HIS PROMISE:
"Through the praise of children and infants, you have established a stronghold against your enemies, to silence the foe and the avenger." — Psalm 8:2

"You, dear children, are from God and have overcome them because the one who is in you is greater than the one who is in the world."— 1 John 4:4

Beyond the Rut

"No eye has seen, no ear has heard, neither have entered into the heart of man, the things which God hath prepared for them that love him."
— 1 Corinthians 2:9

> *The rut we may be in today has no bearing on what God has planned for tomorrow.*

God wants us to see beyond today. Often in the routine of each day, we lose focus on the beauty of the gift of life we've been given. However, the rut we may be in today has no bearing on what God has planned for tomorrow.

So many times, we get caught in the rut of today. A rut is "a fixed procedure or course of life, usually dull or uncompromising." It's going to work, working out, starting a diet again, coming home, chauffeuring children, cooking dinner, going to bed, waking up and repeating. A mental rut will begin to cause us to devalue the beauty of the gift of life today.

When I talk to people who've been sick and God has healed them, they never look at a new day the same way. Every day they wake up is a gift from God. They're excited about the little things in the day they didn't take notice of before being ill. They look forward to another day with a grateful heart.

New actions today can change our world tomorrow. New thinking today can dramatically change the direction of our days tomorrow. God wants us to continue to do what we know to do, while He does only what He can do.

Proverbs 2:6 tells us that the Lord gives skillful and godly wisdom, and from His mouth come knowledge and understanding. Often, we don't understand why it appears we're making no progress. God didn't call us to understand, He called us to trust.

God expects us to consistently and faithfully trust Him with each day, no matter how insignificant or dull our days may appear.

While we're doing what we need to do, He has planned significant things to occur in our day. He may have a person we'll meet who will change our career, relationship status, financial position or destiny. God has it *all* planned.

After going through a divorce and being single for 10 years, I had no idea that the day before that tomorrow I would meet my soon-to-be husband, and my life would be forever changed.

It was a typical day just like any other. It seemed insignificant to me. I worked, went to the gym and then home like any other day. Yet God's plan unfolded during my ordinary, same old routine day. There's not one day that's insignificant in His Kingdom. Every day has been planned with purpose.

At this time, I was consumed with my days and my career. Unbeknownst to me, I had a coworker and lifelong friend who had a client who was 92 years old and recognized as the oldest matchmaker in the world. It seems my friend had pre-arranged and finagled me into meeting this little older woman to screen and interview me for a match. I thought the entire thing was ridiculous.

However, on a Tuesday night, I did meet this person. Three days later, I received a phone call from my soon-to-be husband. While meeting for dinner the following evening, it turned out we not only lived only 10 miles apart, but we were also of the same faith and attended the same church. Even our birthdays were 23 days apart. Ninety days later, we were married.

If we rush through each day just trying to get through it, we can miss the gift God has planned for that day, which will forever change our tomorrows.

LIFE LESSON: In the course of our routine days, we never know when God will have a surprise that will change our destiny forever. We have to be looking beyond today because God always has our future in mind.

MY PRAYER: Thank You, Lord, that I don't devalue the gift of today. Please help me see beyond today and know that today holds significant value for tomorrow. Help me to open my eyes and be looking for the things You've planned for this special day.

HIS PROMISE:
"The LORD orders the steps of a good man: and he delighteth in his way." — Psalm 37:23

"Trust in the LORD with all thine heart, and lean not unto thine own understanding." — Proverbs 3:5

Speak God's Promises

"God said, 'I am the Lord. I have spoken; it shall come to pass; I will do it.'"
— Ezekiel 24:14

> *God is faithful to fulfill His promises, but He isn't obligated to fulfill my potential.*

Over the years, I've learned to speak God's promises over my problems. A promise is a "declaration that something will be done or given." It also means "express assurance." God is faithful to fulfill His promises, but He isn't obligated to fulfill my potential.

I'm responsible for pressing into God's promises and fulfilling my purpose. The devil will present every problem imaginable to cause discouragement and keep us from fulfilling our potential.

However, God's Word is our promise. When we speak it out of our mouths, He assures us that our mountains (problems) will be removed from our lives. The promise is on the other side of our mountain. Our potential is on the other side of God's promise.

The number one thing that will keep us from our potential being fulfilled in our lives is the fear factor. Fear will not only paralyze us from moving forward, it contributes to the results of our circumstances.

Fear will bind our minds and release words from our mouths that contradict God's promises for our lives. As a result, our mouths can override our outcomes. When I control my mouth, Satan can't control my life. There's a promise from God for every problem.

When I was in lack in any area of my life, I would say to the Lord, "You said in Philippians 4:19 that You would supply all my need according to Your riches in glory by Christ Jesus."

When I was single and desired to be married, I spoke God's

promise over my life — "Lord, You said in Psalm 68:6 that You set the solitary in families. You also promised You would bring those who are bound into prosperity. I'm single and need financial provision, so thank You for my husband and Your provision."

When I've had an injustice done to me and felt manipulated, I would speak God's promise to my injustice — "Lord, You promised in Psalm 37:27-28 that if I would turn from evil and do good, then You will not forsake me, and my wrongdoers will be destroyed."

There's nothing that God's promises won't cover. Mark 11:23 says it best. "I tell you the truth, you can speak to this mountain, 'May you be lifted and thrown into the sea,' and it will happen. But you must believe it will happen and have no doubt in your heart. I tell you, you can pray for anything, and if you think that you've received it, it will be yours!"

We have to *speak* to our mountains and *believe* that the power of God's Word will remove them from our lives. When I'm overwhelmed with circumstances, injustice or altercations in relationships, I'm reminded that there's not one mountain that God's promises can't remove. When we speak God's promises to our mountains, He's faithful to remove them from our lives.

LIFE LESSON: Every problem that exists is covered by a promise from God. The condition of our lives are subject to the promises we declare and believe.

MY PRAYER: Thank You, Lord, that You are faithful to perform your Word. Please help me speak to my difficulties and not rehearse them with my mouth. Amen.

HIS PROMISE:
"He was fully persuaded that God had the power to do what he had promised." — Romans 4:21

"The LORD said to me, 'You have seen correctly, for I am watching to see that my word is fulfilled.'" — Jeremiah 1:12

Hearing God's Voice

"My sheep hear my voice, and I know them, and they follow me."
— John 10:27

> *The constant state of being busy causes us to not be able to hear His still, small voice.*

One trick of the enemy is he makes us think we don't hear the voice of God. A voice is "an expression in spoken or written words that expresses approval or disapproval." We learn to hear God's voice through reading in the Bible what God's Word says.

The words in the Bible are God's words. We know His character and how He acts and reacts in situations. We understand what He approves of and doesn't. Most importantly, we learn God's love is unconditional. His love is not based on what we do, but on who He is.

When we press in and seek God, He gives us the confidence to hear Him. When we're prompt in action when we hear and trust Him with our lives, we will make wise decisions that lead us to peace.

Proverbs 3:7 tells us, "Do not be wise in your own eyes; fear the LORD and shun evil." This is rather simple and to the point; however, I have to remind myself that God is more intelligent than I am and to stay away from people and places that don't honor Him. When I thought I was smart enough to figure out something independently, I realized that I wasn't as bright as I thought.

There have been times in my life where I was frustrated, thinking I couldn't hear God's voice. To hear, we must be still. The constant state of being busy causes us to not be able to hear His still, small voice. Even a small child can hear the voice of God.

When my granddaughter was seven years old, she asked me, "How do you hear God's voice? I can't hear God-talk." I said that we listen to the voice of God by reading the Bible so we can recognize the voice of Jesus when He talks to us. It works the same way she hears the voice of her mommy and daddy.

For example, when we were young children, our moms and dads began to tell us to brush our teeth before going to bed, pick up the toys off the floor, don't chew with our mouths open, share our toys with others, treat others like we want to be treated, always be kind, etc. They start telling us these things when we were babies so that those principles would be in our minds and hearts.

When we're alone and in a situation where all our friends are gossiping about a little girl and being mean to her, we hear our mom's voice in our heads saying, "Be kind and treat her how you would want to be treated if that were you."

My granddaughter looked at me and said, "Oh, like when I was at my other Mimi's house, and I was chewing my ice. I heard my mommy's voice in my head say, 'Don't chew ice. It is bad for your teeth.'" Then she looked at me and said, "I do hear God's voice."

When we read our Bibles, the words we read and put into our hearts will be deposited and eventually come to our minds in the middle of a dilemma. When someone is rude to us, we hear "Love is patient; love is kind; love is never harsh." God *does* talk to us. When we read our Bibles, His voice enters our minds, drops into our hearts and gives us the confidence to follow through and obey what we hear.

Be encouraged — God *is* talking to you right now.

LIFE LESSON: We must spend time with God in His Word to recognize His voice. What we hear from Him will always be in line with His character. When we're prompt to obey without hesitation, we can have victory in every situation.

MY PRAYER: Thank You, Lord, that I hear Your voice. Help me remember that in order to recognize Your voice, I must spend time in Your Word. When I put Your Words in my mind and heart, You will always talk to me throughout the day. Help me to slow down so I can hear You when You speak to me. You give me the confidence to make the right choices and decisions. Amen.

HIS PROMISE:
"When the Spirit of truth comes, he will guide you into all the truth, for he will not speak on his authority, but whatever he hears, he will say, and he will declare to you the things that are to come." — John 16:13

"But he said, 'Blessed instead are those who hear the word of God and keep it.'" — Luke 11:28

Love is a Decision

"If you love me, keep my commandments." — 1 John 14:15

> Love is a
> commandant,
> not an option.

When people talk about love as an *option*, I've found it difficult to understand. There's no option about love. Love is a decision — one *chooses* to love. 1 John 4:19 says, "We love because Jesus first loved us."

When we were in our worst condition, Jesus chose to love us. He decided to live on earth and die for us to know His deep love. Over the years, I've heard so many couples say, "We fell out of love" or "We just don't love each other anymore." Love is not a feeling; it's a decision.

First Corinthians 13:8 states, "Love never fails." God is love and He *never* fails. We're a product of God. His love in us will never fail, which is hard to grasp, but it's the truth. When two people join together in matrimony where God is truly the center of their relationship, their love will not fail.

We can fail each other, but love decides in advance not to quit no matter what; therefore, love never fails. Romans 8:31 states, "If God is for us, who can be against us?" This is good news. If we have no other thing in a relationship to agree about, that's a good start. God is for our relationship so that we can make it work with Him by our side.

Over the years, I've seen children and parents choose not to love by their actions and communication. In addition, I've seen friends who've had friendships end, never speaking again after years of bonding.

In the past, I had a dear friend for many years. After much hardship in her life, she chose to, in simple words, not follow Jesus anymore. Her decision caused me to love her from a distance. I couldn't go where she was going.

However, sometimes the greatest love is loving from a distance. I never quit loving, praying and believing she would find her way back to Jesus. Yet, I didn't go where she chose to go.

The best way to show love is to love our families and friends even when they don't deserve it. Over the years, I'd contact my friend and gently witness, but she didn't want to hear it. It was painful to experience, but we can't force love.

I could've chosen not to love my friend anymore, but I decided to love her from a distance. I learned that she too was watching me from a distance. I never quit loving and she never quit watching.

She watched my life and its consistency. In addition, she watched me love her unconditionally no matter what. Although we didn't hang out, I never dropped her out of my "friend status." Every year, I sent her a Christmas card, with a letter to keep her updated with my life. Until recently, I never knew how much those cards and notes meant to her.

It's the little things that speak volumes. The cards meant to her that I was still her friend. She knew I wasn't supportive or in favor of her backward slide, but she knew her choice didn't affect my choice to love her. She believed in Jesus, but she wasn't following Him. To believe isn't enough; we must also love. Today, I'm grateful to say my friend loves Jesus with her entire being.

Satan also believes in Jesus and knows who He is. That's why he fights us on every side to walk away from Jesus' love. The devil knows that Jesus is all powerful and His love is the controlling factor of all things. And he wants to separate us from Jesus so that he can disarm our love, causing us to lose control of our lives. But love is a commandant, not an option.

When we *decide* we're committed to Jesus, we'll show we're committed to His love. When we don't love all the way, we'll eventually lose our way.

LIFE LESSON: Behind every decision to not love is the result of not being committed to loving unconditionally. Love has no strings attached. When we're committed to Jesus, we're committed to demonstrating His unconditional love to those around us.

MY PRAYER: Thank You, Jesus, that You love me unconditionally. My decisions — good or bad — have never affected Your deep love for me. Amen.

HIS PROMISE:
"If a man says, I love God, and hates his brother, he is a liar: for he that loves not his brother whom he has seen, how can he love God whom he has not seen?" — 1 John 4:20

"Love the Lord your God with all your heart and with all your soul and with all your mind and with all your strength. The second is this: Love your neighbor as yourself. There is no commandment greater than these."
— Mark 12:30-31

It's Not What You See

"And we know that all things work together for good to them that love God, to them who are the called according to his purpose." — Romans 8:28

> *Regardless of what we see or feel, it makes no difference to the truth of God's Word.*

When I don't see change, it doesn't mean change isn't taking place. Just because I don't feel like anything is happening doesn't mean that something isn't happening. So many times, what I see and feel try to persuade my feelings to agree with my circumstances. I've learned that the times that appear to be bad are often much better than they look.

The devil will make us think it's over. He will tell us, "This time, there is no way you will make it. This is your final outcome," which are lies.

I can remember when everything in my life was spinning out of control and unexpected — my brother died at 29 in a car wreck, my sister died at a young age from illness, my former husband left me, my mom moved away and my life spiraled in a different direction. All unexpectedly. When things happen suddenly, without warning, it can throw our emotions off balance.

My feelings and emotions were out of control and my life was totally out of control. My future looked and felt anything less than promising. However, Jeremiah 29:11 says, "'For I know the plans I have for you,'" declares the Lord, "'plans to prosper you and not to harm you, plans to give you hope and a future.'" I clung tightly to this Scripture.

My life appeared to be dim and gloomy. It didn't look like I would prosper and I certainly didn't feel hopeful. The truth is it all turned out for my good. For awhile, things didn't look good or feel good. However, for the first time, I honestly had to come face-to-face with things in my life that were out of my control. Finally, my dependency was on God and God alone.

Although I had a heart for God, I had no idea that I hadn't released full reign of control of my life over to God. As a result, I discovered how things look and feel when they have no bearing on the reality in God's Kingdom.

God judges everything according to His Word. God divides the truth from lies, right from wrong and good from evil. His Word required me to see my life as He sees it. He sees me walking in victory. However, it was up to me to walk toward the victory line, despite the obstacles along the way.

Regardless of what we see or feel, it makes no difference to the truth of God's Word. God will work out all things for our good. It's amazing when things go wrong how we have a hunger for life to be right.

When we become desperate for the truth, it's then, and only then, that God, the righteous one who sees with His sovereign vision, can guide us out of the darkness and back into His light.

LIFE LESSON: God's Word has *final* authority over my life. The times that have appeared to be the worst in my life have been the times that have drawn me the closest to God and His truth. The truth of God's Word set me free, and whoever is set free is free indeed.

MY PRAYER: Thank You, Lord, that You see things as they actually are. When it starts getting dim in my world, Your Word is a light to my life. Help remind me that You have my life in control and that everything that has breath responds to Your divine authority, including me. Amen.

HIS PROMISE:
"Study to show yourself approved unto God, a workman that needs not be ashamed, rightly dividing the word of truth." — 2 Timothy 2:15

"The grass withers, the flower fades, but the word of our God stands forever." — Isaiah 40:8

Press In

"I press on toward the goal to win the prize for which God has called me heavenward in Christ Jesus." — Philippians 4:13

> *The devil wants us to give in, but God wants us to press in.*

If I want something bad enough, I must be willing to press in to receive what I desire. The devil wants us to give in, but God wants us to press in.

My daughter played high school and college basketball. In basketball, they would do what was called a full-court press. It was a defensive style where the defense plays man-to-man or zone defense to put pressure on the offensive team. Some presses attempt to deny the initial inbound pass and trap ball handlers in the backcourt. That same pressure applied in a basketball press is what we need to do when Satan tries to apply pressure to keep us from obtaining all that God has planned for our lives.

We need to press into God and deny Satan access into our lives. Pressing into God traps the enemy in the backcourt, denying him entry. When we experience loss, the devil makes us think it's over, but that's not so. In God's inner court where the devil has no access, we have access to provision.

God's throne is in the inner court, providing us protection, love and security that gives us the confidence to go forward without fear. No weapon the enemy uses to try and penetrate can break through the court of His throne of grace.

His Word says we can come boldly to His throne of grace and obtain mercy and help in our time of need. When we press into God, it pressures the devil, causing him to lag because he doesn't have access to the inner court of God's great provision and love. Where the presence of God is, the devil must flee and leave us be.

LIFE LESSON: When the devil tries to press into our lives, we need to press into the inner courts of God's great grace. Where pressure abounds, God's grace abounds greater.

MY PRAYER: Thank You, Lord, that when the devil tries to apply pressure, I can press into Your Word and enter Your courts with praise. You can deliver me from any pressure that would try and come into my life. Amen.

HIS PROMISE:
"Let us then, with confidence, draw near to the throne of grace, that we may receive mercy and find grace to help in time of need." — Hebrews 4:16

"Enter into his gates with thanksgiving and into his courts with praise." — Psalm 100:4

Supernatural Provision

*"And my God will meet all your needs according to
the riches of his glory in Christ Jesus."* — Philippians 14:19

> *God wants us to push
> through the normal, go
> beyond and enter into a
> realm that defies
> natural laws.*

Being brought up in a middle-class family, I was never pushed to go beyond what I'd grown accustomed to. We were never without, but we never experienced abundance. What we become accustomed to evolves quickly into what we relate to.

We relate to the familiar rather than what's unfamiliar. Faith requires stepping forward without seeing while trusting God for our next step. The devil tries to keep us trapped in the familiar so we'll not step into the abundant life God has prepared.

Throughout my life, it seems that an unfamiliar territory with most people, Christians included, is the supernatural. The supernatural is defined as "being above natural or unexplainable by natural laws."

God wants us to push through the normal, go beyond and enter a realm that defies natural laws. When the world says, "no way," God has a supernatural way that supersedes all odds. The supernatural isn't some spooky thing; it's how God operates. God's way overrides man's method. When the odds of my life were against me, I was thrilled that God was for me.

When the doctors gave me a bad medical report, God superseded it with a good report. When I was single, the world said, "All the good men are taken." I was ecstatic when God said, "I have a handpicked man just for you." When the devil said, "You're finished," I was grateful God said, "You will finish your race." Now I'm celebrating a life of supernatural abundance when the devil had told me, "You'll never amount to anything."

When we allow our natural state of mind, natural circumstances and natural provisions to enter into God's supernatural thinking and supernatural way of doing things, we'll enter a place beyond and above any experience — an abundance of God's supernatural provision.

LIFE LESSON: There's a logical way to man, but God's ways aren't logical. They're supernatural. If I can dare to believe in a supernatural God, I will dare to demonstrate His power that will supersede all odds.

MY PRAYER: Thank You, Lord, that I don't have to accept any sentence the devil gives me. If Your laws supersede gravity, it will supersede my circumstances. Thank You that today I receive the supernatural provision You desire to provide. Amen.

HIS PROMISE:
"For as the heavens are higher than the earth, so are my ways higher than your ways, and my thoughts than your thoughts." — Isaiah 55:9

"There is a way that seems right to a man, but its end is the way of death (way of the devil)." — Proverbs 14:12

Jesus Cares

"Casting all your care upon him, for he careth for you." — 1 Peter 5:7

> The best
> demonstration of Jesus
> is to look for ways to
> act like Jesus.

One day, my husband and I invited an Asian woman from my nail salon to church with us. We were excited that she accepted the invitation. Throughout the entire service, she wept. Then she shared a touching story with us.

In her country, as a small child, her family was impoverished. She said we couldn't understand the level of poverty in her country — the average person lives on $10.00 a month. When she was 15 years of age, her parents sent her to a different part of the country so she could work by day and go to school at night. Her aunt lived in a nearby village and found a job for her sweeping the grounds of a hotel.

Being only 15 years of age and far away from her parents, she was lonely and scared. Because of her poverty and lack of dental care, she had lost her front row of teeth. This made her feel even more lonely, insecure and ugly. However, the hotel director took notice of her plight, taking her under his wing. He took her to a dentist and had her front row of teeth replaced with beautiful white veneers.

After some time, her aunt died. Now she was truly alone with no family nearby and no place to live. Again, the hotel director stepped in, finding her a place to live. In addition, he made sure she was taken care of. She couldn't comprehend why he would do this for her. After all, she was a young, poor girl with no way to repay him. She tucked his generosity and love in her heart and vowed she would never forget his kindness.

At the age of 21, she moved to the United States. She married a man who would eventually become a wealthy CEO of Mars Incorporated (M&M's). Sadly, her husband died of cancer. Again, God made sure that she was well cared for, as her husband left her financially set for life.

She often thought about the man who was so generous and loving to her when she was a young girl. She had no idea if he was living or not, but she couldn't get him off her mind. One particular day, she asked her sister to inquire if anyone knew if he was still alive in her country. She found out that he was 88 years old and financially broke. He had retired from the hotel; however, in retirement, his wife became ill with terminal cancer and was sick for 13 years. His wife's illness depleted his resources. When she died, he was left with expensive medical bills, and no way to pay them.

After receiving his address, my friend sent him a card telling him she was the "little girl with no teeth" from his past. He remembered exactly who she was. She promptly paid all his medical bills. Shortly after, she went back to her country to see him, buying him new clothes and food as well as giving him extra money to put in the bank. After all these years, he couldn't believe this "little poor girl" was in a position to pay his bills, and that she took the time to thank him.

During her visit, she told him about Jesus and that He cares. She explained to him that Jesus was caring for her by placing him in her path when she was a frightened little girl, and that Jesus cares about him as well. This old man would have never listened to her, but he knew there was no way a poor little girl from his past could have ever repaid him for the teeth, let alone his extreme medical bills. She decided to take him to church, where he accepted Jesus. The last time she checked on him, he was 90 years old and still living for Jesus. Now he knows that only Jesus could have seen to it that a *poor little girl* could become rich, and a *poor old man* could become whole.

LIFE LESSON: Jesus cares. He's always watching over us. The best demonstration of Jesus is for us to look for ways to *act* like Jesus. What we do for the least of our brothers, Jesus will do for us.

MY PRAYER: Lord, help me never to overlook someone who needs a touch from You. The best way to show Your love and care is to help someone who can't help themselves. Thank You for caring for me. Help me to care for others by showing Your love. Amen.

HIS PROMISE:
"The King will reply, 'Truly I tell you, whatever you did for one of the least of these brothers and sisters of mine, you did for me.'" — Matthew 25:40

"As for me, I am poor and needy, but the Lord takes thought for me. You are my help and my deliverer." — Psalm 40:17

Open Doors

"Ask, and it will be given to you; seek, and you will find; knock,
and it will be opened to you." — Matthew 7:7

> *I've learned that the key is to knock on the door, not knock the door down.*

All things are possible with God. Regardless of the past, God can and will open new doors. He can also open doors that no man can shut.

The most unexpected and memorable events that've taken place in my life were God-ordained doors He provided for me to walk through. He opened the door to meet my husband, incorporate my business, begin our ministry and enter financial success.

Typically, if you want to enter through a door, you would knock first and wait for someone to open it. Matthew 7:7 tells us, "Ask, and it will be given to you; seek, and you will find; knock, and it will be opened to you."

In my life, there have been many occasions where I would pray about a situation. In desperation to get what I prayed, I would knock the door down before I knew God was on the other side. After desperately wanting to find love after betrayal and tragedy in my family, I would pray the Lord would send me a godly husband. It seemed I'd know early on in my spirit whether the person I was dating was the man or not. If not, I would continue to justify how he possibly could be or could one day change.

When we know that something *is not right*, that's a door God *is not opening.* Sometimes I have been fearful of walking in a door, and other times I have charged through, uninvited by God. I've learned that the key is to knock on the door, not knock the door down myself.

Fear of not getting the results we want is a master tactic of Satan, keeping us from knocking on the door and waiting on God to open it. In desperation, I've prayed and knocked. When the door didn't' open right away, I pushed my way in. The results were never

167

good.

Through painful experiences, I've gained the wisdom to know when the door doesn't open, God has a reason — it's to protect us. It could be the wrong time or place or perhaps the wrong person. But if the door is right, God will confirm it by standing at the door to greet you.

When I was forming my corporation in January 2007, we were in three states and barely on the map in our industry. During the entire year, I confessed that it would be a year of God's favor like never before with doors flinging wide open that no man could open or shut. Every day of 2007, I made this my confession.

In October 2007, a door was finally opened, which enabled us to compete with all the big players in the industry. In the next three months, we acquired over 500 clients and grossed more in those months than the entire year.

Within the next few months, we expanded into 12 states. Under natural circumstances, we should've never had that opportunity, but God opened the door and we walked through.

When God opens doors, His favor ushers you in. Today, our marketplace ministry is in 50 states and we have over 30,000 clients. The original door that opened is still a revolving door of new clients. We give God all the glory.

When we begin to recognize that God alone is our source and trust Him for provision in every area of our lives, we'll see doors flying open that'll cause us to enter in and launch us into the next season of our lives.

LIFE LESSON: We must trust God to open and shut doors in order to have a fruitful life. God is the key to every success in life. His key alone can open and shut a door permanently.

MY PRAYER: Thank You, Lord, for opening new doors. Remind me to continually be seeking You and knocking. I know that if You open the door, it'll be securely open. If You shut a door, it's for a reason, and it'll be shut securely as well. As I wait to see new doors open, help me to shut any doors that would hinder my walk. Amen.

HIS PROMISE:
"He who is holy, who is true, who has the key of David, who opens and no one will shut, and who shuts and no one opens." — Revelation 3:7

"I have put before you an open door which no one can shut, because you have a little power, and have kept My word, and have not denied My Name." — Revelation 3:8

It Doesn't Matter

"For we are God's workmanship, created in Christ Jesus to do good works, which God prepared in advance for us to do." — Ephesians 2:9-10

> *God's love isn't based on what we do or don't do. It's based on who He created us to be before the foundation of the world.*

Growing up, my family appeared to be the perfect "Leave It To Beaver" family, which was an old television show about the ideal family. The father always got home in time for dinner, the mom always cleaned the house wearing a dress and pearls and the children always learned their lesson by the end of the show. It was a picture-perfect, all-American family.

As a young girl, my family appeared to be the perfect modern-day family. My mother worked at J.C. Penney, a department store, while my father was a postman who served in the military for 21 years. I was the perfect student, taking honors classes and graduating at the top of my class.

Every Sunday, my mother took us to church. Every night, we ate dinner as a family and prayed over our meals. However, there was one thing missing — a father. Although my father was physically present, he merely existed. I had a loving and supportive mother and was grateful for a dad who provided, but he wasn't a part of our lives.

My dad was what I would call a responsible alcoholic. He worked every day, came home, laid in his recliner and drank himself to sleep. Night after night. When I was a young child, my dad had served in the Vietnam War and was never the same when he came home. In essence, I had an absent father. He disengaged himself from life, only going through the motions. I had a deep desire for a daddy to love me, hold me and be proud of me. At an early age, I learned the art of overachieving.

Most overachievers strive for some acknowledgment or recognition. In my case, it was a father. Not knowing a dad's love often diminishes our heavenly Father's love for us. God's love isn't based on what we do or don't do. It's based on who He created us to be before the foundation of the world.

This concept is hard to wrap one's mind around. He has already done all He will ever do. It is finished. God said in Jeremiah 29:11, "'For I know the plans I have for you,' declares the LORD, 'plans to prosper you and not to harm you, plans to give you hope and a future.'" Our only requirement is to *receive* God's best and *believe* His plan for us will come to pass no matter how it appears to be. It's so simple, yet it seems complicated to comprehend that it doesn't matter who we are or what we may have been through. Despite our circumstances, God still has a promising future for us.

Once I learned that I didn't have to strive for my heavenly Father's attention but receive His Love, I was able to receive His provision, comfort, healing, wisdom, influence and inheritance. No matter what our families looked like in the past or look now and no matter our circumstances, when we receive the love of Jesus, our past doesn't matter anymore. His love changes everything.

LIFE LESSON: It doesn't matter what life appears to be. It only matters that God has planned a beautiful future for us and Jesus died to set us free.

MY PRAYER: Thank You, Father, that though my past doesn't matter, I matter to You. Your grace and love are always unconditional. My job is to receive Your love as You love me unconditionally. Amen.

HIS PROMISE:
"For it is by grace you have been saved, through faith — and this not from yourselves, it is the gift of God — not by works, so that no one can boast." — Ephesians 2:8

"See what great love the Father has lavished on us, that we should be called children of God." — 1 John 3:1

Intentional Thinking

"May these words of my mouth and this meditation of my heart be pleasing in your sight, Lord, my rock, and my redeemer." — Psalm 19:14

> *We must avoid allowing our feelings to dictate our thinking.*

Years ago, I suffered the pain of betrayal in my previous marriage. The image of this other woman with my husband dominated my thoughts. In return, these thoughts controlled my feelings, days and eventually my entire life.

I continually rehearsed the possible outcome and how it would affect my future. I meditated on these negative thoughts day and night to the point that they became a detriment to my health. Romans 12:2 says, "Do not conform to the pattern of this world but be transformed by the renewing of your mind. Then you will be able to test and approve what God's will is — His good, pleasing and perfect will."

We must avoid allowing our feelings to dictate our thinking. We must focus on renewing our thoughts with God's plan for our future. Jeremiah 29:11 states, "'For I know the plans I have for you,' declares the Lord, 'plans to prosper you and not to harm you, plans to give you a hope and a future.'"

If I ever want to have a life with an intended purpose, I must intentionally put Scripture in my heart and renew my thinking. The devil deliberately fills our hearts and minds with the negative; therefore, our focus is on the negative. God wants us to intentionally place His Word and truth in our hearts and minds so we can focus on His goodness. If we neglect God's Word, which is good news, from entering our minds and hearts, we'll begin to adopt human reasoning and focus on the negative the world displays. God wants us to focus on His goodness, which overpowers the world's ugliness.

When we guard our hearts with God's truth, He'll guard our

lives with His goodness. What we allow our minds to think will eventually reveal the lives we're living. When we fill our minds with Christ-like thoughts, we'll have Christ-like lives. What I allow my mind to think about is a choice and my choice alone, which requires discipline. However, even amid betrayal, the more I chose to guard my thoughts, the more I began to see I would be alright; God has a future planned for me and it will be good.

What goes in our hearts will eventually be manifested in our lives. Out of the abundance of our souls is what is produced in our lives. All thoughts have a price. Good thoughts are seeds that produce value. Bad thoughts are seeds that produce only destruction.

The truth of God's Word that we meditate on will reveal the truth of the lives we choose to live. If we want to live lives of excellence, we must intentionally choose to think excellent thoughts. The results of good thinking are well worth the effort. When I began to change my thoughts, it eventually changed who I became and the life I lived. If I find my life in a place I'm not satisfied, I have found my thoughts were not thoughts that would produce satisfaction.

LIFE LESSON: If we want to think right, it is necessary to know the truth of what is right, so we can live the excellent lives Jesus died to give us.

MY PRAYER: Thank You, Lord, that today I have a choice to honor You with my thoughts. I choose to reject negative thoughts and release them with Your truth. Help me discipline my thought life, so my life will reveal Your goodness. Amen.

HIS PROMISE:
"Finally, brethren, whatsoever things are true, whatsoever things are honest, whatsoever things are, whatsoever things are pure, whatsoever things are lovely, whatsoever things are of good report; if there be any virtue, and if there be any praise, think on these things." — Philippians 4:8

"You keep him in perfect peace whose mind is stayed on you because he trusts in you." — Isaiah 23:7

God's Favor Changes Everything

"May the favor of the Lord our God rest on us; establish the work of our hands for us — yes, establish the work of our hands." — Psalm 90:17

> *There isn't anything that God's favor can't or won't do for the person who recognizes His favor is available.*

The favor of God can do what I can't. In the past, I've been in many situations where only God's favor was able to explain the outcome. The more we get to know the character of God, the more intimately we understand that He desires to pour out His favor on us to be equipped to live successful lives.

In my earlier years as a Christian, I realized that it wasn't just my determination and hard work that were moving my life forward, but it was the favor of God. My persistence to make things work out the way I wanted was never enough for lasting change. The more I recognized God's favor, the more He demonstrated His favor in my life.

God responds to a grateful heart. First Thessalonians 5:18 says, "In everything give thanks." So even when I get favor with a front row parking space, I give God the glory by saying, "Thank You, this is the favor of the Lord." Even though this is a small thing, I need to understand that God's willing to give me favor in small things so I can have confidence to rely on His favor in the big things.

God's favor can change the outcome of a court decision, reverse mindsets, open positions we're not qualified for, restore severed relationships, find ways to bring money in when money is nowhere to be found and change the direction our lives are going. There isn't anything that God's favor can't or won't do for the person who recognizes His favor is available.

LIFE LESSON: There may be times when it looks like there's no way out, but when you experience the favor of God, everything is subject to change.

MY PRAYER: Thank You, Lord, that there is nothing that Your favor can't change. Thank you for Your favor on my life. Amen.

HIS PROMISE:
"And Jesus increased in wisdom and stature, and in favor with God and man." — Luke 2:52

"Surely, LORD, you bless the righteous; you surround them with your favor as with a shield." — Psalm 5:12

See it in Your Heart

"I pray that the eyes of your heart may be enlightened so that you will know what is the hope of His calling, what are the riches of the glory of His inheritance in the saints." — Ephesians 1:18

> The essential key to believing is seeing what you believe in your heart isn't only true, but it's so.

Over the years, I've realized that agreeing with God's Word and believing God at His Word are two different things altogether. I can agree mentally in my head (mental assent) that God said it and it's a true statement, yet not believe it in my heart.

As a child growing up, watching my parent's relationship was quite ordinary. Their marriage and commitment to each other were nothing exceptional. It was nothing special — simply a married couple going through the daily routine day after day. They woke up, kissed each other goodbye, came home and kissed each other good night. That was what I saw. I never witnessed affection, love, passion, admiration, adoration or honor for one another.

As a teenager, I dreamed of having a beautiful marriage with a husband who loved and adored me. I didn't want an average marriage, but an exceptional marriage.

When I found in God's Word that He would grant my heart's desire if I would commit my ways to Him, I became committed to His Word. I knew in my heart He would be faithful to deliver His promise.

Matthew 6:33 states that if I will seek God first and His way of doing things above all other things, He would take care of my desires and needs. I only have to commit my ways and believe. The essential key to believing is seeing what you believe in your heart isn't only true, but it's so. I had to *see* my husband in my heart before I would ever see him manifest in my life.

However, the most challenging part for me was trusting while I waited. If we genuinely believe God will deliver what He's promised, we can patiently trust Him while we wait.

In my heart, I had such a vivid picture of my future husband. Even when it looked like I would never find him, I knew deep in the depth of my being that he was on the way. The best way to get doubt and uncertainty out of our heads and faith into our hearts is spending time daily in the Word that supports what we believe in our hearts.

The most tremendous encouragement I can give anyone believing for a mate, a better marriage or a relationship is to have a clearly defined picture that's supported by God's Word. Don't waiver on what you're believing for God to manifest. He will manifest it.

Draw a line in the sand and don't cross it. Satan will try to make you compromise and rush. He makes you think the clock is ticking and time is being wasted. Don't worry about wasting time away; God will make it up to you.

For 10 years, I waited for my husband. When we met, 90 days later we were married. Now that's supernatural acceleration. It has been abundantly above and beyond anything I could've dreamed or imagined. Ever since we married, I've been on the adventure of my life. He was worth every minute of every month and of every year that I had to wait. It's much easier to make boundaries in the beginning in order to avoid being heartbroken in the end.

When we have a clear picture in our hearts and the devil presents you with the wrong person, you'll recognize it. When we know who we're looking for, it's much easier to identify them when they come. If I have a purpose in my heart that I'm willing to wait for, regardless of how long it takes for God's best, it will not take long.

Be encouraged — It's worth the wait to receive God's best.

LIFE LESSON: When I believe God for something in my life, the quicker I get a vivid picture in my heart, the faster I'll see it manifest in my life.

MY PRAYER: Thank You, Lord. You're faithful to Your Word. Help me to see clearly what You've seen all along. As I stand believing, help me to be patient to wait for Your promises to come to pass. Amen.

HIS PROMISE:
"But as it is written: 'Eye has not seen, nor ear heard, nor have entered into the heart of man the things which God has prepared for those who love Him.'"
— 1 Corinthians 2:9

"Now faith is the substance of things hoped for, the evidence of things not seen."
— Hebrews 11:1

Hope

"But those who hope in the LORD will renew their strength.
They will soar on wings like eagles; they will run and not grow weary;
they will walk and not be faint." — Isaiah 40:31

> *God's plan is for us to be so desperate in the middle of our hopelessness that we find Him.*

Reflecting on my life, I've seen a pattern of God's greatest work in my most challenging and seemingly hopeless situations. When the devil presents his lie wrapped in a pretty package and ties it with a bow, don't unwrap his lie.

He knows our weak spots and will look for opportunities to present deception so we will accept it as truth. When he finds a weakness such as money, anger, lust, insecurity, loneliness or jealousy, he'll capitalize on every opportunity. Every time, he'll present the same dilemma wrapped in a different scenario.

When I was single and struggling, the devil would take every opportunity to make sure I was presented with an unexpected financial dilemma that would require an immediate need for money that I didn't have. It left me feeling insecure as a mother and ultimately hopeless.

When I was in my 20s with a small child, I literally couldn't afford to put gas in my car. I was in a continual panicked state to make ends meet. I clearly remember getting out of my car to put the small number of coins I had to put gas in my car. As I looked down, there was a $5.00 bill laying on the ground next to my car. It may not sound like much, but that $5.00 caused my faith to grow. God provided for me when I was unable.

The Bible says if we have faith as small as a mustard seed, we can move mountains (Matthew 17:20). It's incredible how a little glimpse of hope can cause our faith to grow into a massive flaming fire. As a result, this caused me to understand Matthew 6:26 better. "Look at the birds of the air; they do not sow or reap or store away

179

in barns, and yet your heavenly Father feeds them. Are you not much more valuable than they?"

When I had the revelation of God's deep love and provision for me, it became more manageable not to accept the devil's lie when he came to present it again. I replaced the devil's lie with God's promise for my life.

Through reading God's Word, He wants us to join with Him in our battles against the enemy so that our case may be acquitted (declared not guilty). The devil will always present his case — the problem at hand — and try to make us take a plea bargain of guilty. Why should I plead guilty as charged by the devil, when Jesus already paid my debt to set me free? God will provide a way out in the middle of the wilderness. We only need to be brave enough to put our hope in Jesus.

The devil's plan is for us to be so desperate that we lose all hope. God's plan is for us to be so desperate in the middle of our hopelessness that we find Him — the Prince of hope.

LIFE LESSON: The devil's assignment is to make life difficult and seemingly hopeless, but God's continually showing me that there's no situation too desperate when we trust in Jesus.

MY PRAYER: Thank You, Jesus, that You're Lord over my life. You've already paid the price for all the tricks and schemes the devil presents. Thank You that I don't have to fight a battle that You've already won. Amen.

HIS PROMISE:
"*May your unfailing love be with us, LORD, even as we put our hope in you.*" — Psalm 33:2

"*You will not have to fight this battle. Take up your positions; stand firm and see the deliverance of the LORD.*" — 2 Chronicles 20:17

Exhaustion

"For which cause we faint not; but though our outward man perishes, yet the inward man is renewed day by day." — 2 Corinthians 4:16

> *When I feel burned out or stressed out looking for answers, I've concluded that the answer isn't somewhere out there, but inside me.*

When we get to the point that we wake up tired and go to bed tired no matter how much we try to get rest, we're exhausted. It's a sign that our spirit is worn down. To exhaust means "to empty the contents." It's when we're depleted or drained completely. Simply put, there's nothing left to give.

We can't expect to put out more than what goes in. The Bible says though our outward body may perish, our inward body is being renewed day by day (2 Corinthians 4:16).

God never intended us to do good, be good, look good and feel good without daily washing and renewing our minds. It's imperative to read our Bible and soak in God's love and wisdom daily.

Too often we're so consumed with maintaining schedules that we don't slow down and spend quiet time alone with the Lord. It's like not taking time on a road trip to stop and get gas. It may appear you're making good time and going farther. However, when you run out of gas, the time you thought you saved is lost, and the frustration will spiral and ultimately cause regret.

We need quality time each day with the Lord. The Bible tells us we're to seek God first and His way of doing things, then all the other things that concern us will be personally taken care of by God (Mathew 6:33). If we're not mindful, we can spend our quiet time searching for answers and pleading with God. However, God is desirous of one thing — relationship.

When I'm spending time with my husband, it's for one reason. I desire him. I choose him over anyone else. I don't want anything from him. I want him to be near and to be with him, enjoying his company. I'm not looking for answers, only his companionship.

The Lord desires our fellowship as well. Through intimate conversation, we'll gain wisdom and find the answers we're searching for. The strength we need each day is in our inward man. It's in our spirit where Jesus resides and where all wisdom comes from.

James 3:17 tells us, "But the wisdom that comes from heaven is first of all pure; then peace-loving, considerate, submissive, full of mercy and good fruit, impartial and sincere." To paraphrase, God will give pure advice with no partiality or hidden motive. We can trust it's in our best interest. Then, in the end, we will bear fruit (good results on our behalf).

When I feel burned out or stressed out looking for answers, I've concluded that the answer isn't somewhere out there, but inside me. The more intimate time I spend with God, the more energy and wisdom I acquire to do greater things for Him.

LIFE LESSON: I can't give out more than I take in. When pressure arises and life weighs us down, it's time to evaluate if we're "doing" for God or "being" with God. Being with God is always the better choice.

MY PRAYER: Thank You, Lord, that when I become tired and overwhelmed with my schedule, I never get too busy to spend time with You. In Your presence, I will find rest. Amen.

HIS PROMISE:
"Come to me, all you who are weary and burdened, and I will give you rest."
— Matthew 11:28

"Do not be conformed to this world, but transformed by the renewing of your mind." — Romans 12:12

Determined End

"For the Lord God of hosts will make a determined end
in the midst of all the land." — Isaiah 10:23-25

> *In the proper context, determination can be good if Jesus is the anchor of our souls.*

I'm a determined person. If people tell me it can't be done, I'm the type of person who will try to prove them wrong. I'm all too familiar with obstacles and have become accustomed to not letting them deter me. Throughout my life, I've always been determined to make it. I've believed deep in my heart, even during times of disappointment, betrayal and pain, that Jesus will never let me down.

In the proper context, determination can be good if Jesus is the anchor of our souls. The devil has often tried to take my absolute resolve and use it as fuel to ignite pride. Sometimes in my firmness of purpose to finish my race strong, it has caused me to strive instead of rest in Jesus.

Before Jesus came into my life, I was determined to be good, do good and feel good. The more committed I became, the more opposition the devil caused. When I learned Jesus had already determined my beginning from my end, it was much easier to turn my determination into a platform of immovable faith.

It's overwhelming to wrap our minds around the fact that the moment God created the foundation of the world, before our parents ever met, before we were even a thought, before we took our first breath, God had pre-determined our lives. He knew what we would do with our lives — who we'd date and eventually marry, the career we'd choose, how many children we'd have, and that we would spend our lives serving Him.

God had it all planned. He also knew what it would take to live in this fallen world, the tragedy I would experience, the pain I would endure, the love I would find and the faith my journey would require. I continually remind myself: it's okay, things are not that big of a deal in the scope of eternity, this too shall pass, hold your tongue, all things are possible and there's no lack in the Kingdom. God has pre-determined my life, so I've determined, why stress at all? I might as well enjoy my life on the way to where I'm going.

LIFE LESSON: There's nothing we'll ever go through, experience, or do that will change God's mind about our destiny.

MY PRAYER: Thank you, Lord, that You care enough about me that You planned my life. Remind me, that there's nothing I can do that will change my destiny if I trust You each day. Amen.

HIS PROMISE:
"Before I formed you in the womb, I knew you. Before you were born, I set you apart for my holy purpose." — Jeremiah 1:5

"'For I know the plans I have for you,' declares the LORD, 'plans to prosper you and not to harm you, plans to give you hope and a future.'"
— Jeremiah 29:11

Walk by Faith

"For it is by faith we walk, not by sight." — 2 Corinthians 5:7

> *We can't be stuck in yesterday and think we'll advance today.*

Faith declares the outcome before the fight of faith ever begins. In my walk of faith with God, I've discovered that I always win. The first principle I ever learned was to walk by faith. In the Christian arena, walking by faith has become a cliche that many say, but fail to walk out daily.

When we walk, we're advancing. We have one foot on the ground. With each step, we take new ground. Taking new ground is the key. We can't be stuck in yesterday and think we'll advance today. When we're grounded in faith, it's the foundation or basis of where our beliefs and actions rest. We believe by faith that with God all things are possible. By all means, nothing is impossible with God. We know the outcome — we win.

If God is for us, who can be against us? If God is for us, how can we lose? If I declare in the beginning what I'm believing and never give up my ground, God, in His faithfulness, never lets me down.

We often make the mistake of looking at what we see and deciding that what we see isn't looking so good. The result of walking by physical sight is that we lose spiritual vision and inevitably lose ground. Faith never walks by sight. Faith walks by what God's Word says. We see through the eye of our circumstances; God sees through the eye of faith. Hebrews 11:1 says, "Now faith is the substance of things hoped for, the evidence of things not seen."

We believe before we see, which requires faith in God to deliver His promise. Isaiah 55:11 says, "So shall My word be that goes forth out of My mouth: it shall not return Me void, but it shall accomplish that which I please and purpose, and it shall prosper in the thing for which I sent it." We can always have confidence in

God's Word.

When we give Satan permission to take ground by our thoughts of doubt, we're declaring loss. I heard a 105-year-old preacher say, "When you're on God's side, you're always on the winning side." Therefore, we need to decide in advance, regardless of the outcome, to trust God. I don't permit myself to go to the other side of what I believe. I must find in God's Word what He has promised for my life. Then, I must stand. Ephesians 6:13 says, "When we have done all we know to do; stand!" That means I believe what the Bible says. I won't move off God's promise until victory has manifested itself.

When I believed God for my husband after a devastating betrayal and divorce, I decided in advance God was for me. I had to determine there was love after betrayal. I had to declare that I'd love and trust again and my life would be good again. We must believe God is for us. Always. The devil wants us to believe that after hurt, disappointment and temporary defeat we can have a second chance, but we have to settle for second best, which is a lie. With God, we can go from glory to glory. It's not just good, it gets better. No matter how our lives may appear, when we walk by faith, God gives us assurance that what's in front of us will be better than what we left behind.

LIFE LESSON: It's a decision to walk by faith. If I decide in the beginning, according to the promises of God, that nothing is impossible all things will become possible.

MY PRAYER: Thank You, Lord, that today I choose to walk by faith. I declare in advance that I'm going to win my battles. You've promised me in Your Word that we can call things that are not yet. Therefore, I declare that I have victory.

HIS PROMISE:
"I make known the end from the beginning, from ancient times, what is still to come. I say, 'My purpose will stand, and I will do all that I please.'"
— Isaiah 46:10

"God gives life to the dead and calls into being." — Romans 4:17

Remain in the Game

"Therefore, my beloved brethren, be steadfast, unmovable, always abounding in the work of the Lord, since you know you do not labor in vain."
— 1 Corinthians 15:58

> *If we remain in the game, God will see to it that we experience fulfillment despite our circumstances.*

When things go astray and suddenly life is interrupted with unexpected heartbreak, tragedy or disappointment, we have to make up our minds to be all in and remain in the game. There are so many opportunities to check out and not be all in. Even though I've experienced betrayal, tragedy, loss, sickness, lack, physical and verbal abuse, death of siblings and parents, failure and abandonment, I choose to remain. God will sustain.

He will support us, hold us up and bear our burdens. If we remain in the game, He'll make sure we'll be changed and win. It's our choice to be all in. When my life would've been easier to sit on the sidelines and watch, I had a choice to remain. It's a choice only I could make. I could either live my life half-hearted or I could be all in. Philippians 4:13 says it best — "I can do all this through him who gives me strength." With Jesus by our side, we can do this.

In college, my husband played football and loved the game. There was an interview with an injured player who was still playing. He said, "I'd rather play in pain and remain in the game than sit on the sidelines and watch the game being played."

Too many times, the devil tempts us to sit on the sideline and watch our lives go by as we nurse our wounds. I've found I can nurse and rehearse all my failures and hurts or I can get in the game and push past my pain. Athletes are often injured. Yet, they bandage up and remain in the game.

When my sister went home to be with the Lord unexpectedly at a young age and eight weeks later my dad passed after a massive heart attack, I watched my mom make a choice. She chose to remain in the game and continue to live.

In my life, my mom was an example and a rock. Watching her remain during a season of pain, inspired me to remain when I experienced seasons of pain. We need to remember there're always people on the sidelines watching the ones in the game. I watched my mom face each day head on as she chose to remain. She kept going with a good attitude, even from day one.

Finally, I asked my mom how she did it. Aren't you hurting? She said she was hurting and felt pain, but she made up her mind to get up every day and put one foot in front of the other and let God do the rest. We all have good and bad days, but she embraced each day and chose to live life to the fullest to the best of her ability.

What she was saying was she chose to remain in the game of life. It's not in our strength, but by God's spirit in us that gives us the strength to go on. We must wake up and live despite injury or pain. If we remain in the game despite our circumstances, God will see that we experience fulfillment.

To remain means "to continue in the same state." God wants us to continue in the same state of trusting Him with our hearts. He wants us to remain steadfast and unmovable as He comforts, loves and guides our steps each day. If we have breath in our lungs, then God's not finished with our lives. The Bible says we're to go from glory to glory with life getting better and better. The devil wants to convince us that our best days are behind us, which isn't true. Our best days are ahead of us.

God works out all things for our good. We only have to love Him enough to remain in the game. Tragedy, death, unfaithfulness or loss can't hold back God's goodness and purposes for our lives. However, we need to remain in the game, pushing through the pain and choosing to remain. As we continue to remain, God shows His unconditional, steadfast love.

Even though I lost two siblings, all my grandparents and my parents at a young age, I remained. As a result, God multiplied my family. My daughter and son-in-law have given me the gift of eight beautiful grandchildren.

Even though I had unfaithfulness in marriage, I chose to remain. As a result, now I have a husband who's a man after God's heart and loves me wholly and tenderly beyond anything I've ever known.

Even though I lost my home and belongings in a fire, God has blessed me today with a house beyond my wildest expectations or dreams.

I'm grateful that I decided to remain and trust God with my life. It's a choice. We can either sit on the sidelines and watch life go by or we can remain and live lives we never expected. It's all because God honors those who choose to remain.

LIFE LESSON: When we choose to remain, God will strengthen us to stay in the game. It doesn't matter how we feel or think; it only matters that we trust God enough to sustain us as we remain.

MY PRAYER: Thank You, Lord, that You give me strength to go on when I feel like sitting on the sidelines. You're my strength and hope and I trust in You. I know that sometimes it hurts to go on, but help me to remain steadfast as You work out all things for my good. I trust You enough to go forward and stay. Amen.

HIS PROMISE:
"God is love, and whoever remains in love remains in God and God in him."
— 1 John 4:16

"'Not by might nor by power, but by My Spirit,' saith the Lord of hosts."
— Zechariah 4:6

Perfection

"So be perfect, as your heavenly Father is perfect." — Matthew 5:48

> I'd confused the spirit of excellence with the spirit of perfection, which means pride.

Mac Davis, a country singer, wrote a song with the following lyrics — "Oh Lord, it's hard to be humble when you're perfect in every way." For many years of my life, the *attempt* to be perfect was a stronghold.

In the third grade, my bow had to be tied perfectly and my dress needed to have no wrinkles. If these two things didn't happen, I'd take them off and change clothes. When I was in seventh grade, if my hair wasn't perfect, I'd rewash it before leaving for school. In high school, if my paper didn't have perfect cursive, I'd tear it up, after it was finished, and start all over.

As an adult, my perfection caused me to judge others for their imperfection. I'd confused the spirit of excellence with the spirit of perfection, which means pride.

Although I had a spirit of excellence, the devil quickly seized the opportunity to pervert that spirit into a spirit of perfection. All of this resulted from a tiny seed of pride to be perfect, which was planted by the devil when I was a child.

That's what the devil does. He twists the things of God to destroy our purpose. How accurate the lyrics above are — it's hard to be humble and perfect at the same time. To be perfect means "to be free from any shortcomings." Humble means "to be free from the independence of our will."

Often our shortcomings and weaknesses were meant to be our greatest strengths. We have to have the patience to develop the gifts God has given us. I'm grateful I've learned that the grace of God makes me sufficient in my weakness. It's in His power that makes all things perfect in my time of need. Now, I don't strive to be perfect, but try to humble myself to be perfected in Him in every way.

LIFE LESSON: If we humble ourselves before God and submit our independence to Him, He will take our shortcomings and lift us above our circumstances. He's the one who makes us perfect and complete in Him.

MY PRAYER: Thank you, Lord, that I don't have to strive to be perfect. Instead, I need to humbly submit to You in my weakness and allow You to perfect my situation through Your strength. Amen.

HIS PROMISE:
"Humble yourselves in the sight of the Lord, and he shall lift you."
— James 4:10

"My strength is made perfect in weakness. Therefore most gladly, I will rather boast in my infirmities that the power of Christ may rest upon me."
— 2 Corinthians 12:9

Words Matter

"The tongue has the power of life and death,
and those who love it will eat its fruit." — Proverbs 18:21

> *When I'm going through difficult times, I've learned to stop and listen to what's coming out of my mouth.*

A few years ago, the Lord spoke in my spirit this powerful truth — "Watch your mouth, and I'll move your mountains." There's power in the words we speak. Early in my walk with the Lord, I learned the power of words.

The old nursery rhyme that says, "Sticks and stones may break my bones, but words will never hurt me" is a big fat lie. Words not only have the power to hurt us, but also the power to destroy.

When I become overwhelmed, it's tempting to let idle, futile (ineffective and useless) words roll out of my mouth. Words shape or break our lives. Over the years, God has been patiently teaching me that if I want a powerful, abundant-filled life, I must speak words filled with the power and abundance of His Word to back them up.

God has lovingly shown me that I must look to His Word to determine my life, not my circumstances. When I look at my situation square in the eye, it can appear grim and hopeless. When I look at God's promises square in the eye, everything looks different and better.

Ephesians 1:18 says, "I pray the eyes of your understanding may be enlightened so that you may know the hope to which he has called you, the riches of his glorious inheritance." When the eyes of our spirits see what God sees, we begin to see the hope and purpose He has for our lives.

God's Word brings clarity; the devil's lies distort vision. When I'm going through difficult times, I have learned to stop and listen to what's coming out of my mouth. My mouth must be in agreement with God, not in agreement with what I see, which is the devil's hope and plan. I place God's promises in my heart and speak them out of my mouth until the power of God's Word changes my circumstance.

When I believed God for my husband, I found Scriptures to back up His promises to fulfill them in my life. I would say, "Lord, Your Word says, in Proverbs 18:22, 'He who finds a wife finds a good thing and obtains favor from the Lord.' Help my husband find me. You know where I am Lord, so bring him to me. That scripture carried incredible power in my life. In the end, God did bring him to me form Florida within 10 miles from where I lived.

God will do whatever it takes to change our lives through the power of His Word. His Word is the key that unlocks His promises. Any dead, hopeless situation can be brought to life if we put God's Word in our hearts, speak it out of our mouths and believe it until we see it manifested in our lives.

Romans 4:17 says, "We are to call the things that are not as they already were." That is speaking in the faith of God's promise over our lives. When we oppose His Word by complaining about what we currently see in our lives, this is what the Bible refers to as being double-minded, which cancels out faith.

No matter what we face and no matter how it may look, God always has a way out. There's power in His Word and He is faithful to deliver His spoken Word in our lives. If we can watch our mouths, God will remove our mountains.

Be encouraged — Find God's promise that will speak to your mountain and watch Him move it out of your life.

LIFE LESSON: When we speak out of our mouths what we see with our eyes, we get precisely what we see. When we speak out of our mouths what God's Word says, we get exactly what God sees.

MY PRAYER: Thank You, Lord, that Your Word produces life. Please help me not to speak dead words over my life. Any dead and hopeless situation can be brought to life if I believe You at Your

Word. You're faithful to move every mountain in my life. Amen.

HIS PROMISE:
"Truly I tell you, if anyone says to this mountain, 'Go, throw yourself into the sea,' and does not doubt in their heart but believes that what they say will happen, it will be done for them." — Mark 11:23

"For the word of God is quick, and powerful, and sharper than any two-edged sword, piercing even to the dividing between soul and spirit."
— Hebrews 4:12

Step Again

"The LORD makes firm the steps of the one who delights in Him."
— Psalm 37:23

> *It's not the wrong step that will keep us in our past, but the "step again" that will bring us into our future.*

It's not what we turn away from, but who we turn toward that begins to define our lives. It's when we turn away from our past and step into God that our lives take a different turn. Our future is grander than our past. Thank You, Jesus.

Satan lives in the past because he has no future, but *we do*. Our past is nothing more than a reminder that our loving Savior has redeemed us to bring us hope for our future. Our past is something that has *formerly* been, not *currently* is. My past has been a stepping stone for my destiny. When we step forward, we move by lifting our foot and setting it down again in a new position, not an old position.

Notice that a step requires us to lift up our feet again. We may make a wrong step along the way; however, it's not the wrong step that will keep us in our past, but the "step again" that will bring us into our future. We have to trust God with our next step, which requires us to believe our next step will be secure when our last steps were insecure.

If we allow Him to guide our steps along the way, they'll be securely ordered of the Lord. In Psalm 40:2, the psalmist says, "God has placed his feet on a rock and makes his footsteps firm." We can trust God. I can recall times when I'd failed due to placing confidence in myself, which made it challenging to have confidence that I would not fail again.

After the worst year I ever experienced, I remember the fear of stepping out again. It was the year my children were going away to college and we had just built our dream home. However, eight months after we moved in, my 35-year-old sister had kidney failure

195

and suddenly went home to be with the Lord.

A few short months later, I accidentally stumbled on a letter from another woman to my then-husband only to find out they'd been having an affair for four years. The shocking news was they were planning on getting married. My confidence, image and security were shattered in one moment — in one letter —, which soon led to a divorce.

The good news is that we have a Savior who loves us. We're not to have confidence in our ability to step out again, but God's ability to lead our steps. It's the "again" that will get us to where God had planned for us all along.

Step again. Once more. Another time. Yes, a new step and opportunity to get it right. God is a God of second chances. Even though I've failed so many times in my life, God didn't fail me. My choices brought me to a failed outcome, but God's always faithful to take my failure and turn it into His victory. I thank God that He doesn't give me just one chance to get things right. If I turn away from my past and turn toward God, He'll show me if I step again, it will be worth it.

LIFE LESSON: The more we trust God to take the next step, the more secure we'll become to step again. It's not the last step that will define our lives, but the next step that allows us to get it right.

MY PRAYER: Thank You, Jesus, that You give me the courage to step again when the last step didn't go as I'd planned. If I trust You to step again, You're faithful to lead my steps. Today, I trust You with my steps, as I know they're ordered of the Lord. Amen.

HIS PROMISE:
"He brought me up out of the pit of destruction, out of the miry clay, and He set my feet upon a rock making my footsteps firm." — Psalm 40:2

"You enlarge my steps under me, and my feet have not slipped." — Psalm 18:36

Time for Change

"To everything, there is a season, a time for every purpose under heaven."
— Ecclesiastes 3:1

> *When we become complacent and accept defeat, it becomes a snare intended to hold us permanently hostage.*

I've sometimes found that life forces us to make a change. Years ago, when I was married and my former husband left our family, moved to a new state and started over with a new wife and life, I was forced to make a change. To be forced means "an involuntary act that demands a change."

Even though it wasn't what I wanted, if I didn't accept change my life would never change. My life would've remained in the same position — going nowhere. If I lived in the memories and regrets of yesterday, I would've been in a sad place, not enjoying the beautiful life God had given me today.

Unfortunately, many brothers and sisters are still living in the graveyard of their past. John 11:1-44 gives the account of Lazarus being raised from the dead. He'd been dead for four days. When Jesus arrived at his tomb, He said in a loud voice, "Lazarus come forth." In verse 44 it goes on to say, "The dead man came out, his hands and feet wrapped with strips of linen and a cloth around his face. Jesus said to them, 'Take off the grave clothes and let him go.'" Jesus has the power to resurrect *any* dead situation. However, we can't go forward when we're bound in grave clothes.

Second Corinthians 5:17 says, "Therefore if any man is in Christ, he is a new creature: old things are passed away; behold, all things have become new." I've known friends whose past died years ago, yet they refuse to move on. Maybe they don't want to let go and embrace change. Change is never easy when it isn't something we initiate. It means life will be different from what it was initially. It's not only uncomfortable, it's unfamiliar.

So many times, I've convinced myself that change was transpiring out of my failure, which is defeated thinking and straight from the devil. Defeated thinking convinces us that the best is behind us. When we become complacent and accept defeat, it becomes a snare intended to hold us permanently hostage. It causes us to remain in yesterday and not press into today. When I get to a place where my physical, mental and spiritual state is content to "be as is," I'll never grow to be all Jesus created me to be. Jesus wants us to press in and move forward, continually pressing to finish our race strong. Certain events in my life — either by force or choice — have brought new opportunities that advanced my position.

Whether you're going from high school to college, one state to another, single to married or barren to with child, it's all a part of life that'll bring about change. God created us to change. Every year as we grow older, even our physical looks change, which is a natural process of metamorphosis. God has a spiritual process of metamorphosis as well. If we allow the change of natural circumstances to draw us closer to Jesus, we'll grow in strength, courage and love. As we trust Him in the process of change, it'll reshape our lives to be exceedingly abundantly better than we could ever dream or imagine.

LIFE LESSON: There's a season and time for everything. There's a season to sit still and a season to move forward. There's a season to remain and a season to gain. However, through every season, Jesus is the *same*. He'll never leave us or forsake us. His love remains steadfast and true forever.

MY PRAYER: Thank You, Lord, that I accept change as a vital and necessary part of growth. As my life changes, help me to embrace You in order to make it through the shift victoriously. Amen.

HIS PROMISE:
"Jesus Christ the same yesterday, and today, and forever." — Hebrews 13:8

"Be strong and courageous. Do not be afraid; do not be discouraged, for the LORD your God will be with you wherever you go." — Isaiah 41:10

Tell Your Children's Children

"Tell it to your children, and let your children tell it to their children and their children to the next generation." — Joel 1:3

> *We're not dwelling on what we haven't yet accomplished, but instead on all God has already accomplished in our lives.*

When we speak words out of our mouths, we give birth to thoughts that drop in our hearts. If we're not careful, instead of giving birth to faithfulness we can begin to breed forgetfulness. It's so easy to "arrive" and forget where we were before we got there.

One day as I was thanking God for our beautiful home and His goodness, I was reminded of exactly how far God had brought me. Instantly, I remembered the small two-bedroom house with one bathroom and no shower or closet. If Jesus could be born in a messy animal shelter and placed in a manger with no place to lay His head, I could live with no place to hang my clothes. I was grateful for everything I was given.

Deuteronomy 4:9 says, "Only take care, and keep your soul diligently, so you do not forget the things that your eyes have seen, and do not let them depart from your heart all the days of your life. Make them known to your children and your children's children." Simply meaning, let our children know and see all of God's faithfulness and goodness He's poured out on our lives.

Psalm 37:3 says, "Trust in the LORD, and do good; dwell in the land, and feed on His faithfulness." When we remember where we once were and praise God for where we're now, that's feeding on His faithfulness. When we tell our children and grandchildren about God's goodness in our lives, we're birthing gratitude for God's faithfulness in their hearts. We aren't dwelling on what we have yet accomplished, but instead on all God has accomplished in our lives.

A few years back, I decided to show our children and grandchildren what God's faithfulness looks like. One Sunday after church, the entire family caravanned three cars to my hometown of Weatherford, Texas. As we slowly drove down the old familiar street where I used to live, tears streamed down my cheeks and my heart was overwhelmed with God's faithfulness. At that point in my life, I never dreamed in my wildest imagination the big dreams God had for my future. At that point, I was trying to survive, barely making ends meet. Yet God had huge plans for my destiny that I had no idea about. If we don't give up, God won't disappoint.

As we pulled in front of the old house, my heart was overwhelmed with gratitude. As we all stood and looked at the weathered old home, images of struggle and barely enough flooded my thoughts. I wasn't sure what the people inside thought as so many people stood gazing at their home. As I knocked on the door, an older woman answered. I told her I used to rent this home and how special it was to me. As I asked if it were possible to show my children around the house, she agreed.

To my surprise, the man I rented it from all those years ago happened to be her husband. They were now living in the home he once rented to me. Now in his late 90s, he came to the door. By the grace of God, I was able to share with him how special this sweet home was to me and how it was a memorial stone of God's faithfulness.

They proudly took us on a tour of their sweet home so my children could see God's great love as well as His faithfulness over our lives. They were amazed and surprised that this had once been where I lived. It was exactly how I remembered it. We took pictures with the couple standing in front of my first home and went about our day with hearts full of gratitude to God.

That day, we were all blessed. Our children had a picture of reality of where I came from — a humble beginning. When we begin to think about all we've left to achieve, we need to stop and think about where we came from and where we once were. And we need to tell our children's children of God's faithfulness.

LIFE LESSON: We're to feed on God's faithfulness. When we want to complain about where we are, it's best to remember where we were, as we tell our children and our children's children what an awesome God we serve.

MY PRAYER: Thank You, Lord, for all You have done in my life. Help me to remember that although I may have a way to go yet, You have brought me a long way already. I'm so thankful for Your faithfulness. Amen.

HIS PROMISE:
"Trust in the Lord, do good; dwell in the land, and feed on His faithfulness."
— Psalm 37:3

"Remember this day, in which you came out from Egypt, out of the house of bondage; for by strength of hand the LORD brought you out from this place."
— Exodus 13:3

Concerning Money

"He who trusts in his riches will fall, but the righteous shall flourish as the green leaf." — Proverbs 11:28

> God didn't need my money; He needed my obedience to trust Him at His Word concerning money.

As a single parent, making ends meet was quite difficult. The Bible says we're to give a tithe of 10%, which wasn't easy. To give $10 out of $100 was a challenge since that was all I had to buy diapers and formula. However, God tells us in His Word that every seed produces after its kind.

If we plant a seed, it will produce a harvest. It wasn't easy to let go of the few dollars I earned, but it never failed to amaze me how my small token of obedience blessed me more in my release than in withholding.

When I held on to what I knew I was supposed to release, I would be deficient in making ends meet. The more my heart opened to give, the more God opened the windows and poured out His blessings on my life. While struggling to pay a $250 rent payment on a house, I decided to give a tithe before the rent was paid. It wasn't easy to release even $25 because it took every penny to make ends meet.

However, God didn't need my money; He needed my obedience to trust Him at His Word concerning money. My heart to release what little I had was vital to surviving. My obedience became the very thing that allowed God to pour out His blessing on my life.

On the other side of our obedience is our blessing. The Bible says Jesus humbled Himself and was obedient unto death (Philippians 4:8). His obedience to die for us was the gift we received to live for Him. On the other side of Jesus, obedience is our life.

The more God requires of us, the greater the blessing He has in store for us. As I began to trust God with giving the small amount I had, He increased my money and the bigger my giving enlarged. Today, I'm in awe of the blessings God has poured lavishly on my family. It's all because of God's faithfulness. When we're faithful to give, He's faithful to supply our giving.

Be encouraged — If you have a need, plant a seed and watch God meet your needs in abundance.

LIFE LESSON: God doesn't need our money. He requires our obedience. If we're obedient to give when we're in the "land of lack," God is faithful to bless us in His land of abundance.

MY PRAYER: Help me, Lord, to keep You first and honor You with the money You have entrusted to me. As I give, You are faithful to respond to a cheerful and giving heart. Thank You that Your seed never returns void. Amen.

HIS PROMISE:
"So shall My word be that goes forth from My mouth; it shall not return to Me void, but it shall accomplish what I please, and it shall prosper in the thing for which I sent it." — Isaiah 55:11

"'Bring the whole tithe into the storehouse, that there may be food in my house. Test me in this,' says the LORD Almighty, 'and see if I will not throw open the floodgates of heaven and pour out so much blessing that there will not be room enough to store it.'" — Malachi 3:10

Face the Challenge

"I can do all things through Christ which strengtheneth me."
— Philippians 4:13

> *I've learned God gives His strength to His greatest warriors.*

Challenges can change you, chase you or challenge you. Over the years, I've learned to embrace change that comes from the spoils of the battle. Like many other friends, my life has had significant challenges. Yet, I've always had a strong drive to overcome in the face of a challenge.

Since He created that drive deep inside me, I guess God knew I'd be the one who could handle challenges. When someone challenges someone in a fight, it demonstrates who has the greatest strength and skills. However, in my life, I've learned the greater the challenge, the greater the victory. Years ago, Satan had a death grip on anything and everyone of value in my life. It seemed like when one turned to the book of Job in the Bible, my picture was there.

In one year, my marriage died along with my dog, parents and my sister, leaving me hopeless. I felt I had a death sentence pronounced over me that was irreversible. Everyone I knew and loved was no longer with me. They were gone forever. The weight of the pressure was almost more than I could bear. Yet, through it all, I've learned God gives His greatest strength to His greatest warriors.

First Corinthians 10:13 Amplified states, "No temptation regardless of its source, has overtaken or enticed you that isn't common to human experience, nor is any temptation unusual or beyond human resistance, but God is faithful to His word and will overcome temptation with joy." Therefore, He won't give us more than we can handle.

During that year of heartache, it seemed like God was pushing the envelope with what I could take. Everything in me was screaming, "Stop. I can't bear any more." Of course, God was right as usual. I could and did bear the weight of my challenges. I not only accepted them, but I also was able to rise and live again. The devil plans to make us concede and agree with what we see and feel. He wants us to acknowledge and admit that he has permission to 'take us out" of the battle.

There were days I had to wake up and force myself to get through the day. I never quit my daily routine; however, at times, it was just that — a routine. Sometimes the act of making it through the day was a challenge all on its own. Often the biggest accomplishment of my day was making it through the day.

The good news is God's strength is made perfect in our weakness (2 Corinthians 12:8). When I put forth the effort to wake up each day and place one foot in front of the other and trust God with each step, He would see to it that my steps were firmly planted.

Even though that year was my greatest battle, it was also my most significant victory of overcoming. In addition, it's by far the greatest presence of God I've ever experienced. God manifested Himself in ways that I remain hungry for. Although I wouldn't want to do it all over again, I wouldn't trade the challenge for the world. God manifested His glorious presence in ways that not only will I never forget, but will remain as a memorial of His faithfulness forever.

To this day, I'm still reaping the spoils of that battle. Yes, even today. I have children serving the Lord and a beautiful new family. In addition, I have a God-fearing husband who adores and treasures the gift of our marriage, as well as the courage to continue to face life's battles together. God has continued to remind me that He only sends His greatest warriors to His biggest battles. Big or small, the weight of the challenge is all the same to God.

LIFE LESSON: Challenges can chase you or change you. We have the choice to face the challenge or turn our backs. The battle is for us to lose or the victory for us to win.

MY PRAYER: Thank You, Lord, that I'm able to choose to face the challenges put before me today. Please help me embrace difficulties, unkind people and minor irritations of the day. Then when the significant challenges come, I have the experience to know it's all the same to You. Amen.

HIS PROMISE:

"No temptation (test) has overtaken you except what is common to mankind. And God is faithful; he will not let you be tempted (tested) beyond what you can bear. But when you are tempted, he will also provide a way out to endure it." — 1 Corinthians 10:13

"Greater is He that is in you than he that is in the world." — 1 John 4:4

Faith Activated

"Now faith is the substance of things hoped for, the evidence of things not seen."
— Hebrews 11:1

> *Wisdom says if you don't want your spouse to be in a bar when you're married, don't go looking for your future husband there.*

Over the years, there've been barriers and walls in my life that have come crumbling down. There've been relationships restored, financial barriers broken and walls of separation abolished. A wall is defined as "a hindrance that keeps our victory delayed." Every barrier took one common denominator for the victory — faith. Our faith gives substance to God's Word. When we act on God's Word by standing strong in our faith and refusing to be moved by circumstances, faith will be activated.

When sickness comes, debt is overwhelming or relationships are struggling, it takes faith to trust God will work out all things for our good (Romans 8:28).

When I was single and believing God for a husband, I prayed and immediately put my faith to work. Faith must be accompanied by action. At the time, I wrote out Scriptures on a piece of paper concerning husbands and wives and read them out loud daily. In addition, I wrote a petition to the Lord for the husband I was believing for God to bring me. Then I surrounded myself with men and women of God who had strong faith.

Socially, I went to places that if my future husband were to show up, I'd be proud to find him there. Wisdom says if you don't want your spouse to be in a bar when you're married, don't go looking for your future husband there.

In addition, I thanked God every day for my husband, even when my eyes didn't see him standing in front of me. We can't be passive and merely wait for answers to prayers. We need to activate our faith by acting on God's Word. It doesn't work when we sit back and do nothing. Therefore, we should rejoice before the victory. I used to think sitting still meant waiting for God to perform His Word. However, now I understand it means I do my part, which is all I know to do, while patiently waiting on God to accomplish His part in me and through me.

In Joshua 6, there's a story about the walls of Jericho. The Israelites were to march around the walls of Jericho one time for six days. On the seventh day, they were to march around seven times. When the trumpet sounded, they were to shout for victory. They shouted while the walls were still standing. Anyone can shout praises when the walls are down, but it takes faith to shout when the walls are still standing.

LIFE LESSON: It may look like the walls of my current circumstances are too strong to fall, but if I activate my faith as I trust God while the walls are standing, He'll be faithful to bring them down.

MY PRAYER: Thank You, Lord, that my faith can remove mountains in my life. I'll believe You at Your Word as I go forth and do all I know to do while I wait for victory. Amen.

HIS PROMISE:
"That whosoever shall say unto this mountain, be removed, and be cast into the sea; and shall not doubt in his heart, but shall believe that those things which he said shall come to pass; he shall have whatsoever he said."
— Mark 11:23

"For He, Himself is our peace, who has made both one, and has broken down the middle wall of separation." — Ephesians 2:14

Dark Seasons

*"I have come into the world as a light so that no one who
believes in me should stay in darkness."* — John 12:46

> *The devil's primary target
> when we're going through
> dark seasons is to
> generate a lack of clarity,
> so we're distorted in our
> perception and vision.*

No one wants to admit when
they're going through a dark
season. As a Christian, I can
recall a season of darkness that
made me want to disappear. I
tried to run and hide, bringing
me into more profound isolation
and darkness. I didn't want
anyone to think I didn't have it all
together. What a perfect picture
of pride.

Looking back, I know that it was a seed of deception that
birthed pride. I was embarrassed about the direction my life had
gone. I was an emotional mess. When we go through a season of
darkness, there's a feeling of despair and we become overwhelmed
with no control over the outcome. Darkness is defined as "the
absence or deficiency of light" and Satan is the prince of darkness.
When we're confused, depressed or lacking solutions for our
circumstances, darkness enters to try and consume light.

Darkness causes a lack of enlightenment. The devil's primary
target is to generate a lack of clarity, so we're distorted in our
perception and vision. He wants us to question "why" instead of
trusting God with our why. It's impossible to see our solutions in
the dark, even if the answer is standing right in front of us.

Second Samuel 22:30 tells us that with the Lord, we can fight
against an entire army. In addition, God's Word would be a lamp
unto our feet (Psalm 119:105). We can leap over any barrier or wall
trying to barricade us in from our answers. God's way is perfect,
and the Word of the Lord is proven and is a shield to those who
trust in Him (Proverbs 30:5).

God is our strength and power. When light enters, darkness

must flee. God arms us with strength for the battle, which is good news. He'll subdue under our feet those who rise against us. He'll deliver us from the striving of people and circumstances. It's God who avenges us and suppresses those under us. His Word has power and needs no assistance.

God will cause us to conquer and bring into subjection anything or anyone who tries to get us down. Light overpowers the force of darkness and brings it into subjection to the hand of the Almighty God. The light of Jesus will bring us joy and wipe out depression. Even the darkest season in my life has been my most remarkable testimony. Everything Satan told me that would "not be" is. God is the great I Am.

Death surrounded me, sickness followed my family, love abandoned me and lack hovered nearby to haunt me, but God. He will not fail us. Ever. He's what we need when we need it. Everything in my life that was stolen has been restored 100-fold.

Yesterday, I couldn't pay my bills; today, I'm free of debt. Yesterday, I was betrayed by love; today, I'm happily, blissfully married. Yesterday, my family was taken by sickness, leaving me alone; today, the fruit of our daughter's womb has blessed us with eight amazing grandchildren. Yesterday, I was fearful of tomorrow; today, I anticipate every moment of every day with an abundant life in front of me.

We may experience dark seasons, but if we continue to go forward with Jesus, we'll quickly see the light shining brightly for our future.

Be encouraged — This too shall pass.

LIFE LESSON: Darkness can't live in the light of Jesus. Darkness must flee when light enters in to set us free.

MY PRAYER: Thank You, Lord, for being a light amid the darkness. When I feel I can't see or think straight, remind me that You're a continual lamp unto my feet. Amen.

HIS PROMISE:
"For thou wilt light my candle: the LORD, my God, will enlighten my darkness." — Psalm 18:28

"For God, who said, 'Let light shine out of darkness,' made His light shine in our hearts to give us the light of the knowledge of God's glory displayed in the face of Jesus." — 2 Corinthians 4:6

Prepared and Waiting

"Behold, I am going to send an angel before you to guard you along the way and to bring you into the place which I have prepared." — Exodus 23:20

> *When we question God, we slow down the process. Doubt delays delivery.*

Regardless of gender, I've found that people want to find that special someone who'll be faithful to their hearts, true to their commitment and true to love.

After my former marriage had been compromised, I remember believing God for my future husband. For 10 long years, I waited and longed for love, with no spark of hope for a lasting flame. I felt perhaps that there would never be that "one" special person just for me. There was someone for everyone, so why not me? I would be at conventions, surrounded by 10,000 people at a time, and seemingly everyone was paired up. I would think, "Lord, is there anyone for me?"

Then the Lord said, "Quit looking for who I've prepared for you that you would not pick for yourself." At that moment, that statement was so true. My now husband is the opposite of any man I'd ever dated before. It was as if God was saying, "Why are you looking? Don't you trust that I've gone before you to prepare your way?" Prepare means "to put in proper condition or readiness."

James 1:17 says, "Every good and perfect gift is from God." Before receiving His gift, He wants to prepare our hearts to be in the proper condition to receive it. In my situation, I had to be ready to receive the love He had prepared. When our hearts aren't prepared to receive love, we'll reject the gift of love.

No matter what we're believing God to do in our lives, we'll abuse the gift if we aren't in the proper condition to receive it. God's wisdom knows what we need exactly when we need to receive it. It seems the very things I think I don't want are the exact things I need.

I wanted to be needed; God wanted me complete. I was desperate for my forever mate; yet, God had me patiently wait, needing to put my trust in Jesus. My expectation needed to be in Him and Him alone. I would say with my mouth, "I trust God." However, my heart was saying, "When Lord?" We can't trust God with our mouths with doubt in our hearts. This is being double-minded (James 1:8). When we question God, we slow down the process. Doubt delays delivery.

Today, I'm a living testimony that God has prepared a perfect mate for everyone. I'm not perfect and my husband isn't either, but we've both been handpicked by the perfect One.

Be encouraged — Any gift from God is worth the wait.

LIFE LESSON: We must first learn to trust God's love before we can trust God for our lives. What we're believing, God has prepared and waiting for us to receive.

MY PRAYER: Thank You, Lord, that You have prepared everything I need. Remind me that You have faithfully prepared a perfect plan for my life. I trust You with my life. Amen.

HIS PROMISE:
"Every word of God is pure: He is a shield unto them that put their trust in Him." — Proverbs 30:5

"Sovereign LORD, you are God! Your covenant is trustworthy, and you have promised these good things to your servant." — 2 Samuel 7:28

Ready Vessel

"Preach the word; be prepared in and out of season; correct, rebuke, and encourage with great patience and careful instruction." — 2 Timothy 4:2

> *Too often we have an opportunity to speak into someone's life, and we want to correct when we should love.*

A few years back, I was preparing to leave on a mission trip to Paris. While I was in the airport, God reminded me that He could move in the lives of those we pray for when they least expected it and when we least expected it. Our job was to be *ready*.

We need to be sensitive regarding when to preach, love, instruct or correct. Too often, we have an opportunity to speak into someone's life, yet we want to correct when we should love, preach when we should listen or encourage when we should correct. We should be sensitive and ready in and out of season.

While sitting at a restaurant in the airport with a friend, we were both engaged in deep conversation. When I glanced up, I noticed a middle-aged woman standing in front of our table. As she put down her glass of wine on our table, I thought she was a waitress delivering wine to the wrong table.

Suddenly, I recognized that she was a lady whom I saw in the bathroom, minutes before, standing at the sink texting on her phone. I'd glanced over at her, smiled as I left and told her to have a nice day. Nothing more, nothing less. A simple act, yet a strategic setup by God.

Now here she was, standing right in front of me. All of a sudden, she looked me straight in my eyes and said she wanted to ask me a question. She wanted to know what I would do if I was in a relationship for 14 years and knew the person I was with had been lying the entire time. She said she flew in for the weekend to meet "her" and wanted to know how she should handle it. What a deep, personal question to ask a total stranger. However, when

God wants people to hear His truth, His love has no boundaries.

God drew her in by His Spirit, giving me a one-time opportunity to be His vessel and do and say what He wanted me to do and say. Without missing a beat, I opened my mouth and leaned on God for wisdom. She might not have liked what I had to say, but I said it with God's wisdom. I told her that she should meet with "her" and tell her about loving her and wanting the best for her. However, she should also mention that she knows she has been lying to you the entire relationship, and you're going your own way.

We can't be in a relationship based on a lie. I mentioned to her that the foundation of any relationship has to be based on love, and the foundation of love is truth. Anything other than the truth is a lie and rooted in deception. I continued to tell her that it may be difficult to do, but it'll be worth it. It wasn't the time to rebuke and correct the person she was in a relationship with. God was drawing her in by His Spirit with His love. God had a much better plan for her life.

Keep in mind that this was a profound question to ask a total stranger. Then I gave her an analogy. If someone got shot with a bullet and decided not to have it removed, it would rot and cause problems for the rest of that person's life. If the person chose to have the bullet removed, it would hurt. There would be a recovery period, but it would heal perfectly and never bother that person again. I ended by telling her it took a lot of courage for her to come over and ask that question. God planned this conversation and now she had the wisdom to carry it out.

When she left, my friend said she was praying in the Spirit for me the entire time I ministered. Then we both prayed over her and went our way. How awesome is God.

So many times, God gives us these small but powerful opportunities. He arranges us to plant a seed, water a seed or reap a harvest. We just need to be sensitive and ready. Had I not smiled at the woman in the bathroom and told her to have a nice day, she may not have had the courage to come to my table. It's not our job to correct and point out the error in these situations, but to love and guide people to Jesus.

Even though the relationship was based on deception, I was able to plant a seed that she was in a relationship that wasn't God's best. At the right time, God will use us to minister about the truth of His love, which will direct the person to the proper relationship that God had prepared all along. This was a time to draw her into God's love, not push her away. Ecclesiastes 3:1 says, "For everything, there is a season, a time for every activity under heaven." God has an appointed time for everything.

If God can take a woman sitting at a bar, move her from her seat and have her walk over to a total stranger in the middle of a deep conversation to hear His Word, He can do that same thing at the most unexpected time in the lives of those we love and are praying for.

Be encouraged — God's preparing us as vessels to minister to our families and friends who we're lifting up in prayer.

LIFE LESSON: There's the seed time and there's harvest time. We must be sensitive to plant seeds at the right time, so God can root them in His love and bring the harvest in His time.

MY PRAYER: Thank You, Lord, that You keep our hearts pliable for Your use. Remind us always to be ready to minister Your love as You see fit. We're Your hands and feet. Help us be prepared and willing to speak life into hurting people in a hurting world. Amen.

HIS PROMISE:
"*To everything, there is a season and a time to every purpose under the heaven.*" — Ecclesiastes 3:3

"*We will be instruments for special purposes, made holy, useful to the Master, and prepared to do any good work.*" — 2 Timothy 2:21 NIV

It's all Planned

"'For I know the plans I have for you,' declares the LORD, 'plans to prosper you and not to harm you, plans to give you hope and a future.'"
— Jeremiah 29:11

> *God has set us apart for His purpose. Our misfortunes don't alter His plan.*

God has everything planned for our lives in advance. When I couldn't find my way, I was grateful God didn't leave me where I was. When I was rolling newspapers off a dock at 2:00 a.m. with a baby and utterly miserable with my life, God had bigger plans for my future.

When I experienced the pain of betrayal, I'm grateful He had authentic and genuine love planned for me. When I came out of a devastating divorce, God had a godly man pursuing His heart, preparing to wait for me.

God has gone before us to prepare the way. He has our entire lives planned. Jeremiah 1:5 says, "Before I formed you in the womb, I knew you; before you were born, I set you apart." God has set us apart for His purpose. Our misfortunes don't alter His plan. Thank You, Jesus.

Years ago, when I was a single parent, working two jobs, desperate to provide, lonely and miserable, God knew and planned one day for me to deliver His good news to people around the world. His plans are more than we can ever imagine. Where we may be today isn't what He has for us tomorrow. God never settles for second best. He has bigger and better plans to fulfill our dreams tomorrow.

Be encouraged — God has it all planned and it's good.

LIFE LESSON: In God's eyes, not one moment in our lives is wasted. He has every detail from yesterday planned for us to learn, grow and advance tomorrow.

MY PRAYER: Thank You, Lord, that You have my life all planned. There's nothing I need to do, but rest in today, learn from yesterday and be excited about what You've planned for tomorrow. Please help me to remember that everything I know today will help me grow tomorrow. Amen.

HIS PROMISE:
"Your eyes saw my unformed body; all the days ordained for me were written in your book before one of them came to be." — Psalm 139:16

"But as it is written, eye has not seen, nor ear heard, neither have entered into the heart of man, the things which God has prepared for them that love him." — 1 Corinthians 2:9

Beelzebub

"But when the pharisees heard it, they said, 'This fellow doth not cast out devils but by Beelzebub, the prince of the devil.'" – Matthew 12:24

> *When Satan discovers we've been wounded, it puts a strong aroma of offense into the atmosphere.*

There's safety in the arms of God. In 2000, I experienced total devastation after a surprise divorce. It was Valentine's Day. I came home, fixed a romantic dinner, went to freshen up and change clothes, opened my closet and all my husband's clothes were gone. Divorce papers were in my makeup drawer. Every feeling imaginable came flooding in at once — hurt, betrayal, humiliation, confusion, anger, bewilderment, pain, anxiety, frustration and desperation.

Then the emotional threat that held me hostage rolled over me — fear. Along with all these emotions came unworthiness, undeserving and unbecoming. Although on the exterior, I had it all together, on the inside was a perfect picture of a wounded, fragile and broken heart.

The devil is referred to in the Bible as Beelzebub, which is translated in Greek as "lord of the flies." When I see a wounded animal or bird in the middle of the road, there're always flies all around. Flies love stink, which is nothing more than a strong, offensive smell. The same is true with Satan. When he discovers we've been wounded, it puts a strong aroma of offense into the atmosphere.

When we're wounded with disappointment or pain, we become a prime target for the devil to swarm in and fill our hearts with lies such as "you deserve this, you should've seen this coming, you're not good enough, you'll never be the same, you'll never make it, no one will ever love you again or you'll be alone forever." The deeper the lies penetrate, the deeper we contemplate and give attention to them. However, the truth is that the devil is a liar. He doesn't have a true bone in him. Every lie has a deliberate intention of deception, which clouds God's direction. Deception always deviates from the truth, designing to get us off course.

God not only defends the true and righteous (right standing with God), but He defends the confused and hopeless in their circumstances who put their trust in Him. When I had felt the most unworthy, God revealed to me that I'm worthy in Him and Him alone.

When you know you're not in a place that God wants you to be in your actions and your thoughts, He still loves you where you are. How incredibly humbling. When I was in a state of complete desperation, I found out that the least desirable, needs love the most. And that was me. Desperate people are just that — desperate. When I came to the point where I became desperate enough, my only strength was to utter, "God, You said that Your strength is sufficient, so that's all I have today." In my uttering, God showed up and revealed His unconditional love to me.

His great love is strength in His most perfect form. His love equipped me to endure. His love gave me eyes to see His truth and courage to take another step. His love is sure and sustainable. Even under challenging times, His love remains forever. Be encouraged — You are not alone. God will never leave you.

LIFE LESSON: God's truth always stands. His love remains when everyone else has left us standing alone. In His arms, our ears are close to hear Him whisper, "You're mine. I will never let you go."

MY PRAYER: Thank You, Lord, that although life catches us off guard, You are never surprised. When our hearts are wounded and we hear the devil's lies swarming in our ears, help us to quickly turn and run into Your arms of safety. Amen.

HIS PROMISE:
"Then you will know the truth, and the truth will set you free." — John 8:32

"The eternal God is your refuge, and underneath are the everlasting arms: and He shall thrust out the enemy from before you." — Deuteronomy 33:27

I Decided Yesterday

"Trust in the LORD with all your heart, and do not lean on your understanding. In all your ways, acknowledge Him, and He will make your paths straight."— Proverbs 3:5-6

> *I've learned to determine and settle in advance; I'll trust Jesus with my outcome.*

In my life, I've faced many tough decisions. Having been a young, single parent, I had to decide that I'd be a successful mother and provider for my baby. Losing a brother at age 29 to a car wreck, a sister at 35 to diabetes, a mother to cancer and a father to chronic lung disease, I had to decide that I wouldn't let that weaken my faith in God as my healer.

Having a previously failed marriage, I had to decide that God didn't fail me. As a single woman for 10 years, I had to decide to believe God had the perfect mate handpicked for me. When finances were less than what was needed, I had to decide to believe God was sufficient to meet all my needs. When my children were going through difficult situations, I had to decide that I wouldn't be moved.

If I resolve my controversies and struggles in advance, I've concluded that this helps eliminate torment in the future. By learning to determine and settle challenges in advance, we're able to trust Jesus with our outcome. We have to be persuaded with no reservation that Jesus is working out all things for our good, regardless of what it may appear to look like. One definition of deciding is "to resolve or conclude (a question, controversy, or struggle) by giving victory to one side."

We can either decide to give victory to the devil and agree that what we see is our outcome or we can have victory through Jesus regardless of what we see. First John 5:4 says, "For every one of God overcomes the world, even our faith." As a child of God, we defeat this evil world and achieve victory through our faith. Our faith in Jesus is the victory that has conquered all of our tragedies, heartbreaks and disappointments.

If God is for us, nothing can come against us and have permanent victory. When this world appears to be economically and socially devastated, void of all hope for the future, I've decided to trust Jesus who is the redeemer of it all.

LIFE LESSON: It's not easy to always trust God. However, when we decide in advance that no matter what happens tomorrow, no matter how hard it's to understand or no matter how bad it may appear, we will trust God with today. And we'll find comfort with whatever tomorrow may bring.

MY PRAYER: Thank You, Lord, that You are God, healer, comforter and redeemer for every need in every situation. I trust You today for whatever tomorrow brings. Amen.

HIS PROMISE:
"For I know that my Redeemer lives, and He shall stand at last on the earth."
— Job 19:26

"But blessed is the one who trusts in the LORD, whose confidence is in him."
— Jeremiah 17:7

Circumstances are Temporary

*"He has made everything beautiful in its time. He has also set eternity
in the human heart, yet no one can fathom what God has done
from beginning to end."* — Ecclesiastes 3:11

> *Our pressure will
> pressure us to make
> decisions that are
> usually not in the best
> interest of our long-term
> welfare.*

After a devastating divorce in 2000, my close friends and family suggested moving from my then-current home into a smaller, more manageable one. My former husband and I had just built our dream home on four acres. A few months later, after moving into our dream home, all hell and havoc broke loose in my life.

My 35-year-old sister's unexpected death was more than enough to handle. However, a few short months later the end of my marriage was more than I could bear. The property was breathtaking; however, it required more maintenance than a single, working female could give.

In the process of the pressure to decide for my life, the Lord spoke to me and said, "Don't make a permanent decision while in a temporary situation." Since then, I've always kept those words close to my heart and have leaned into the wisdom of those powerful words.

When life comes hurling in all directions with unexpected events, it can often throw the direction we were going off course. Our pressure will pressure us to make decisions that are usually not in the best interest of our long-term welfare. When tragedy or tribulation present itself, most people feel the need to explain their opinion for our lives. Keep in mind that most people have their best intentions for us in mind, but the one who has the greatest intentions and wisdom is the great one — Jesus.

While contemplating moving from my dream home, I honestly

didn't have peace about it. I felt like I'd be letting Satan win. Why should he take my marriage and my beautiful home? However, I'm sure that if it were the right decision from God, I would've had peace. When it's the right decision, the Lord always give us His peace, prompting us to move forward. The Lord would've given me the desire to move, but that wasn't the case.

Against all odds of what appeared to be the right thing to do, I stayed in the home. Even though it took every Saturday spending seven hours mowing, it was worth the battle to do what I felt the Lord was telling me to do. I refused to make a permanent decision in a temporary situation. Deep inside, I knew there was a purpose bigger than myself to stay and occupy. Oftentimes, the purpose for a decision is revealed little by little, as we move forward in obedience.

A few years later, oil and gas was discovered on my acreage. A pipe was drilled through my property, enabling me to receive royalties beyond what I expected and more significant than most people in my area. And we're still drawing royalties today. Even though it was a stretch to stay, God showed me that He would continue to make up the difference.

At the time, I thought that was my sole purpose for keeping the property. My daughter was in college at the time, but little did I know that years later she would have eight children. She sold her home, and by a turn of events ordained by God, moved into this special sanctuary of a home to raise her children. This was a proper property made for children to run, have freedom and enjoy life. What an awesome God we serve.

God's vision for our lives goes way beyond our temporary situation. When things turn upside down, remember that God has a plan. His plan always sees beyond today, seeing our future in mind.

LIFE LESSON: Our circumstances are subject to change. Today may present the unexpected. However, if we trust God with our temporary situations, He'll take what looks like a mess and make it His ministry.

MY PRAYER: Thank You, Lord, for reminding me that You wrote my life story at the exact moment You created me. You knew what my life would hold from the beginning, and You see the end of my story. Help remind me that You have a beautiful future for me. Amen.

HIS PROMISE:
"'*For I know the plans I have for you,' declares the Lord, 'plans to prosper you and not to harm you, plans to give you hope and a future.*'" — Jeremiah 29:11

"*Desire without knowledge is not good — how much more will hasty feet miss the way.*" — Proverbs 19:2

Comparison

"We have different gifts, according to the grace given to each of us."
— Romans 12:6

> *How often do we find we're comparing ourselves to others when nothing compares to the creator of the universe.*

Before a new year, I asked my husband, if there was one thing I could change to be a better wife in our marriage and a better leader in our marketplace ministry, what would it be. Without hesitation he replied that I should quit comparing myself to others. I objected, responding that I don't compare.

He reiterated that I did, and immediately gave me specific examples: "You comment on people's gifts with an underlying insinuation that your gifts are in pale comparison. You comment on solid leaders with a platform of influence and don't honestly see yourself as one. You admire and respect those in ministry, yet don't see yourself as having equal gifting."

After this conversation, I looked deep into my heart. Comparing myself to others wasn't something I felt I was doing. In my mind, I never let those words come out of my mouth. However, after being honest in my heart, I realized that I did do that.

Even though I never verbalized I wasn't gifted, I didn't see anything of colossal significance in what I was doing. I didn't see my routine day as anything impactful. In my mind, I was just doing what I do. When we're doing our thing, which is our usual everyday routine, we often don't see it as extraordinary, but rather quite ordinary.

Ordinary means "of no remarkable quality or interest; unexceptional." This definition doesn't sound like anything God would create. Extraordinary, on the other hand, means "beyond what is usual." Now that sounds more like the character of God.

His workmanship is exceptional. How often do we find we're comparing ourselves to others when nothing compares to the creator of the universe.

When I press into each day and start with seeking God and His plan for my day, I recognize that it's only with Him that I can accomplish anything. God is faithful to see us through each day. When others watch and see us walk out our days and everyday routine trials while including God in every decision, that's often extraordinary to those looking from the outside in.

It's pressing into every day to what God wants us to get out of each day that makes it exceptional. Too often, we're the ones who make the extraordinary beauty of a new day, and all God has planned, as just another ordinary day.

Be encouraged — God has big things planned for each day. We have to recognize that it takes us right where we are, day by day, to fulfill His plans.

LIFE LESSON: We never know how our everyday routines, with ordinary people watching us handle everyday situations and trials, can be an exceptionally unusual thing for others to witness. We must never diminish the little things; they often have the most significant impact.

MY PRAYER: Thank You, Lord, that You see me as valuable. It's my relationship with You that makes me able to impact people in a way that can only be done with You working through me daily. There's nothing that compares to You. Amen.

HIS PROMISE:
"Nothing compares to the surpassing greatness of knowing Jesus Christ as my Lord, everything else on this earth pales into insignificance compared to knowing Jesus." — Philippians 3:10

"I praise you because I am fearfully and wonderfully made; your works are wonderful, I know that full well." — Psalm 139:14

It's Only a Shadow

"Though I walk through the valley of the shadow of death, I will fear no evil, for You are with me; Your rod and Your staff, they comfort me."
— Psalm 23:4

> The shadow of a dog never bit anyone.

Everything God meant for good, Satan will try to pervert for evil. At every corner, the devil lurks with a dark shadow. When I was 24 years old with two small children, I was in an abusive relationship. Ultimately, I was manipulated and controlled by fear, even fearing for my life.

Psalm 23:4 says, "Though I walk through the shadow of the valley of death, I will fear no evil." Fear of death is terrifying, but the shadow of the Almighty is brighter than the shadow of darkness. Notice that it says we walk *through* the shadow. We don't pitch a tent under the shadow and make it our permanent home. The shadow can't stop us in our tracks or keep us from going forward. Shadow has two completely different definitions. One is "darkness, especially that coming after sunset" while the other is "shelter and protection."

Satan comes immediately after the beauty of something manifested to cast a shadow of gloom, hindering our next step. However, God's shadow provides shelter and protection from the storms. What the devil means for harm, God will turn around for our good. Always. Genesis 59:20 says, "You intended to harm me, but God intended it for good to accomplish what is now being done, the saving of many lives." There's safety under God's shadow.

Leaving the abusive relationship wasn't easy. The fear didn't go away immediately, but the spirit of fear did begin to diminish. Dr. Jerry Savelle, an evangelist and preacher, said, "The shadow of a dog never bit anyone." Satan will make it look worse than it really is. When I dared to say no more and run from the abuse, the shadow, although it wanted to follow me, had no power.

When we feel defeated as a parent, a mate or achieving our dreams and goals, the shadow of failure moves quickly into our thoughts. Second Corinthians 10:5 says, we're to "cast down imaginations, and every high thing that exalteth itself against the knowledge of God, and bringing into captivity every thought to the obedience of Christ."

In addition, Jeremiah 33:3 says, "Call to me, and I will answer you and tell you great and unsearchable things you do not know." Our confidence must come from God exposing the deception of the devil. He'll protect us as He guides our next steps. The only thing that can keep us from having what God says is to allow fear of the shadow to paralyze our faith.

When we put our trust and hope in Jesus with no plan B — or as we say in Texas, "put all our eggs in one basket" — Jesus will fight for us and no harm can penetrate. There's no demon in hell who can cast a shadow that would have any power to affect our lives. When doubt creeps into our minds, we should know it's nothing more than a shadow of deception. Quickly, we should cast the lie out of our thinking and replace it with God's truth. I love reminding the devil that the shadow of a dog never bit anyone; so get lost. Be encouraged — It's only a shadow. God's got this.

LIFE LESSON: It's always darkest before the dawn. It's wisdom to ignore the shadow of the devil and take refuge in the shadow of the Almighty.

MY PRAYER: Thank You, Lord, that I can take refuge under the shadow of Your wing. You are faithful and I trust You, You are my rock and my deliverer. I trust You with my whole life. Amen.

HIS PROMISE:
"He that dwelleth in the secret place of the Highest shall abide under the shadow of the Almighty." — Psalm 91:1

"How excellent is not thy lovingkindness, O God! Therefore, the children of men put their trust under the shadow of thy wings." — Psalm 36:7

Wake Up

*"Awake thou that sleepest, and arise from the dead,
and Christ shall give thee light."* — Ephesians 5:14

> *Once you've awakened,
> you'll have no interest in
> judging those who still
> sleep."* — James
> Blanchard Cisneros

When I was single believing
God for my forever mate, I had
to continually remind myself that
God so loved the world that He
gave His one and only Son. That
was proof enough for me that He
loved me enough to provide me
with my one and only soul mate.

There's not one promise from God that won't cover our lives.
There's not one promise that God won't deliver in our lives.
However, we need to be awake to receive His promise when it
arrives. There's nothing the devil can do to stop us from having the
life God has prepared for us; we only need to awaken and watch
God perform the victory.

We're not required to win the fight; however, we need to stay
awake and be *in* the fight. Good news — we win. It's a fixed fight.
I can recall a time when I was sleeping through life. I wasn't
sleeping literally, but it was as if I was in a bad dream and couldn't
wake up. Then I read a quote by James Blanchard Cisneros that
said, "Once you awaken, you will have no interest in judging those
who still sleep." I understand what it's like to be in a season where
you're numb to life.

The devil convinced me it would be better to exist in a state of
slumber. However, God was calling my name, "Diana arise,
everything is alright, I am with you." From time to time, I remind
myself what it felt like then, which gives me compassion for others
still sleeping through life.

Sometimes it's easier to sleep through the bad times and hope
you wake up when it's all over. Unfortunately, even in times of
discomfort and pain, we have to fight for what we believe. We
must understand that our fight is with the devil, not against people

or problems that arise in our relationships and circumstances. We need not fight the ones we love, but for the One we love.

How do we do that? Since the devil is the source of *all* contention, we must tussle with him. We need to fight the one who is behind everything terrible by activating God's Word. Our weapon of defense is God's Word, which is alive, active and sharper than any two-edged sword. When we're at the point of being caught in a bad dream, it's essential to know that God wants us to come to a state of awareness.

God will take what the devil meant to destroy us to activate our lives again and bring them into the fullness He died to give us. The Lord reminds me often that my life is better than I see. God is continually working behind the scenes.

It's hard to see the good when we continually allow ourselves to focus on the bad. Life never stops happening. However, the good news is that God never stops existing. He never slumbers or sleeps. His Word never quits working. His love never ends.

We may feel inadequate, but God's more than adequate. He's always good. His Word is alive and true. There's no devil, not one, that can extinguish the plans and purposes God has for our lives. Although there'll be battles, we must remember that the battle belongs to the Lord. Therefore, we need to wake up and watch the fight because when it's all said and done and the battle is over, we'll realize we won.

LIFE LESSON: Our lives are worth fighting for. Life can sometimes feel bad, but God is always good. If we can be courageous enough to stay awake and watch the fight, it'll be a fight worth watching.

MY PRAYER: Lord, thank You for strength. You are my defense. Your Word is alive and active. I'm grateful that Your Word has the power and authority to overcome anything. Amen.

HIS PROMISE:

"For the word of God is alive and active. Sharper than any double-edged sword, it penetrates even to dividing soul and spirit, joints and marrow; it judges the thoughts and attitudes of the heart." — Hebrews 4:12

"So then let us not sleep as others do, but let us be alert and sober." — 1 Thessalonians 5:6

God of Completion

"Being confident of this, that he who began a good work in you will carry it on to completion until the day of Christ Jesus." — Philippians 1:6

> *God may take us a different route than we anticipated, but He will get us safely to our destination.*

I'm grateful God didn't leave me where I was years ago when I had no vision for my future and had no idea where I was going. I'm also grateful God had a plan to get me where He'd planned all along.

At the time, I loved the Lord, but never fully understood the faithfulness of Jesus as the author and finisher of my life. I had no idea that what God started in me from the moment I was born He would finish to completion. Hebrews 12:2 tells us Jesus is the author and finisher of our faith. Translated, Jesus *will* finish what He began. If we have the confidence to believe, He's able to see us through until the end.

However, it's easy to lose hope along the way when life interrupts our dreams. Broken relationships, sickness, unexpected misfortunes and the tragedy in our world all contribute to the desire to quit along the way. Our job is to get back up and keep going. God isn't surprised by the things that happen along the way. He still has a plan to complete what He began. It's not up to us to get there; it's up to us to trust Jesus to get us there.

God may take us a different route than we anticipated, but He will get us safely to our destination. Over the years, I've learned that God is able. More than able. Able is defined as "having the necessary power, skill, and resources." God has the power and resources to get us where we're going. It's not up to us to finish His work, but it's up to us not to get weary and quit along the way. He's doing the work in us and through us.

At the same time, the devil strives to wear us down until we give up. God specifically tells us in the Bible not to be weary in doing the best we can every day because if we hang in there, with

Him by our side, we're promised we'll reap a rewarding harvest in the end. The end is to the full extent.

He'll complete in full what He began in us. We can have an earnest expectation that Jesus will finish completing the desires He put in our hearts since the beginning of time.

LIFE LESSON: We can be whole, entire, undivided and complete in every area of our lives — physically, socially and financially, if we believe God will complete in full to the end what He began.

MY PRAYER: Thank You, Lord, that You will complete to the end what You began in my life. Help me keep my eyes on You and not get discouraged or distracted along the way. I know You are faithful. It's You alone who makes me complete and will finish what You began in my life. Amen.

HIS PROMISE:
"Looking to Jesus, the author and finisher of our faith." — Hebrews 12:2

"Let us not become weary in doing good, for at the proper time, we will reap a harvest if we do not give up." — Galatians 6:9

Our Steps are Secure

"The LORD orders the steps of a good man: and he delights in his way."
— Psalm 37:23

> God determines our steps. In return, our steps determine our future.

During a conversation with a dear friend, she mentioned she was anxious about some big decisions that would alter her life. Although she loves the Lord and her heart honors God in every decision, she still feared making the wrong decision. Anytime we have a decision that could alter the direction of our destiny, it naturally causes uneasiness.

The devil loves to paralyze our steps with fear, so we'll not step in any direction. I reminded her that her steps are ordered of the Lord. The divine order of the Lord has predetermined every step we take. It's a simple yet powerful truth. His grace covers our lives. If we desire to please God with our lives and seek His face for direction, His grace will see to it that our feet are firmly planted with every step we take. It's reassuring when we meditate on God's grace.

God determines our steps. In return, our steps determine our future. We have to keep stepping if we plan to reach our destination. Jeremiah 29.11 says, "'For I know the plans I have for you,' declares the Lord, 'plans to prosper you and not to harm you, plans to give you hope and a future.'" When I've made poor decisions, God's grace quickly revealed the error in my steps and turned me around. Before I knew it, my feet were standing on solid ground.

His grace assures us that if we seek His direction while in unknown territory, He will enlarge our path so our feet won't slip. This means God has given our steps grace to step. Even if we step in error, His grace will rescue us and get us back on the right track. When our hearts are turned toward God, we can have the confidence to step out, knowing His grace covers our lives.

It's comforting to know that when we trust God with our steps, we can't make a mistake that will leave a permanent footprint. His grace can change every situation.

LIFE LESSON: There's not one step we take that God won't be there to lead us in our next step or give us the grace to take the first step.

MY PRAYER: Thank You, Lord, that my steps won't be hindered by fear. There's not one step that I take that You don't know I'm about to take. I trust if I step out in error, Your grace will quickly reveal the direction to turn. I trust You with my heart as I step out, knowing I'm secure in You. Amen.

HIS PROMISE:
"The LORD Almighty has sworn, 'Surely, as I have planned, so it will be, and as I have purposed, so it will happen.'" — Isaiah 14:24

"A person's steps are made secure by the LORD when they delight in his way." — Psalm 37:23

It's an Illusion

"For we walk by faith, not by sight." — 2 Corinthians 5:7

> *The illusion of what I saw with my eyes deceived the truth of what God spoke in my heart.*

Satan takes pleasure in painting illusions to get us off course. An illusion is simply "a false leading or misrepresentation of reality." God says in His Word that He will lead us in spirit and truth. What we see with our eyes will deceive us. However, what God says in His Word will lead us into truth.

When things were wrong in my life and there was a tugging on my heart to make a change, there was also a weakness in my flesh, denying me the courage to change my course and move forward with conviction. The illusion of what I saw with my eyes deceived the truth of what God spoke in my heart. At some point, we all battle our will against our spirit.

Our will is what we think or feel we need. God's will is what He has prepared and knows we need to fill our purpose. Ephesians 6:12 says, "For we wrestle not against flesh and blood, but principalities, against powers, against the rulers of the darkness of this world." Therefore, the devil is fighting against us to keep our lives in chaos and confusion so we'll ultimately be unable to make good choices.

When we ignore the tugging in our hearts, we eventually won't hear the whisper of our spirit. I recall a time in my life when I was clearly in a bad relationship. I knew in my spirit it wasn't what God had prepared for my future. However, I couldn't seem to let go of my emotional strings to grab hold of God's spiritual provision.

When we ignore conviction, eventually it turns into condemnation. Conviction is for spiritual correction, which sets us on the right course. However, condemnation is made to condemn and spiral us in the wrong direction. It's all an illusion the devil paints to make us think one thing — everything is okay. When we ignore the prompting of the Holy Spirit, it's not okay. Eventually, life goes back to normal — so we think.

With every passing week and month, I ignored the prompting of the Holy Spirit. I talked myself into believing that everything would be okay, which is all part of his deception. Once again, the illusion produced a false, misleading impression of reality. Things were not okay and they never got better. Ultimately, I was in a relationship that was hindering my spiritual growth.

Satan tries to make us think we're okay outside of God's will. But the reality is we're in danger of God's judgment. We're not judged by how good we are, but by what we've been called to do and how we've been called to live.

It's in God's grace and mercy that He gives us a lifetime to get our lives on course. If we want to grab hold of the reality of God's freedom and abundant provision, we must let go of the illusion Satan has set as a trap to derail our lives.

LIFE LESSON: What I see doesn't mean that's what it is. I'm not to live by what I see and feel, but by the truth of God's Word. In the truth of His Word, I will find reality in my life.

MY PRAYER: Thank You, Lord, that Your Word is true and alive. Your Word exposes the darkness that can cause illusions. Please help me to walk in the light of Your Word. I choose to walk by faith, not by sight. Amen.

HIS PROMISE:
"Lead me in your truth and teach me, for you are the God of my salvation; for you, I wait all the day long." — Psalm 25:5

"Send out your light and your truth; let them lead me; let them bring me to your holy hill and your dwelling." — Psalm 43:3

Don't Ask

"For the Spirit God gave us does not make us timid,
but gives us power, love and self-discipline." – 2 Timothy 1:7 NIV

> *Each time I do what I do, even when I don't feel like doing it, my flesh learns it's not in control.*

Every morning my husband and I get up at 4:00 a.m. to begin our day. As soon as my feet touch the floor, we begin praying together, working out and spending quiet time alone in the Word. This all takes place before we leave for work.

Having a fitness background, I know the importance of working out before becoming too exhausted to fit it into my schedule. I also know this is something that I'm committed to, no matter what. There are no questions asked. It's not an option to not work out. My commitment has developed a no tolerance policy for excuses. It's my responsibility to keep my body as the living temple of God. On so many occasions, I don't feel like getting up early; my body still feels tired. On those days, I most certainly don't feel like working out.

However, I've trained myself to get up and not ask my body if it feels like lifting weights or doing an aerobic workout. I don't hesitate. I just do it.

Galatians 5:17-24 says, "For the desires of the flesh are against the Spirit, and the desires of the Spirit are against the flesh, for these are opposed to each other, to keep you from doing the things you want to do." Even though I may have days where it didn't feel like I had the most intense workout, I still feel victory because I didn't give in to my body's suggestion to skip the workout altogether.

Each time I do what I do, even when I don't feel like doing it, my flesh learns it's not in control. The best way to discipline our flesh — our minds, wills and emotions — is to starve it. If we starve anything long enough, it will die.

239

To starve can be translated as don't give into your feelings. The devil wants us to go by how we *feel*. God wants us to subject our bodies, minds and wills to His will, way and Word. I learned it's not the sporadic hard workouts that make a difference, but the consistent daily workouts that produce results.

The same is true with the Word of God. It's not the time in the Word, but consistently getting into the Word and receiving His truth that produces results. God's Word isn't based on our feelings, but truth, which will teach us to be good disciples. A disciple is translated as a disciplined one. Disciple comes from a Latin word meaning "learner," and discipline comes from the Latin word representing "instruction-knowledge." Instruction and knowledge of the truth come from the Word of God with Jesus as our instructor and us as the students.

We don't question our instructor, but do as He says. Our bodies, minds and wills aren't our master; Jesus is our master. We're to become disciples who do as He instructs, not how we feel. A disciple believes in Jesus, studies His Word and imitates His ways. The devil wants our feelings, emotions and bodies to be the master of our lives.

If I give in to my feelings about my day first thing in the morning, I compromise my day before it even begins. At the very least, if I work out, I've accomplished not giving in to my feelings, regardless of how long I worked out.

When we compromise, we become conflicted. Satan wants us to quit; better yet, he wants us to never begin. When we allow how we feel to direct our steps, we'll always want to take the easy way out and try and make up for it later. For example, we can eat a piece of cake tonight and work out longer tomorrow. However, tomorrow comes and we don't *feel* like working out. Our disappointment about blowing it yesterday punishes us by eating everything in sight today. Compromise leads to regret and consequences.

As a result, I've wasted so much of my time not doing what

needed to be done initially. It's a daily battle of self-talk to not give in to myself, but it's definitely worth the talk. I'm continually learning that although Jesus cares about my feelings, He doesn't want how I feel to run my life. It's wisdom not to ask my feelings what I want to do. The wisdom of God's Word guarantees results.

LIFE LESSON: It's better to do what I don't want to do today in order to have the results I want tomorrow.

MY PRAYER: Thank You, Lord, that when I spend time with You daily, I'm not only being disciplined by You, I'm disciplining my flesh to line up with Your Word, which guarantees results.

HIS PROMISE:
"But I discipline my body and keep in under control, least after preaching to others I myself should be disqualified." — 1 Corinthians 9:27

"A disciple is not above his teacher, but everyone when he is fully trained will be like his teacher." — Luke 6:40

Our Place is Secure

"He made Him who knew no sin to be sin on our behalf, so that we might become the righteousness of God in Him." — 2 Corinthians 5:21

> *Our right standing with God isn't based on what we do, but who Jesus is and what Jesus has already done.*

As a child, I loved going to Six Flags Over Texas. It amazed me that I would stand in long lines for hours for the thrill of a 45-second ride. I didn't ever consider for a moment getting out of line to get a drink or go to the restroom because I would lose my place. If I walked away, my only option was to go to the end of the line.

So many times, I've felt that way with God. I've been doing what I know I'm supposed to do, giving it my all and staying in line with my choices. Then I make a wrong turn, say the wrong thing or get off track. Immediately, I would think that I lost my standing with God. When we make a mistake or make a mess out of our lives, He allows us to ask for forgiveness and have a clean slate. Our place is secure with Him. How awesome is God.

Yet, the devil is always near to whisper lies to us. He wants us to feel the pain of our wrong decision. He wants us to be deceived into believing that we have to *earn* our position with God. He even beats us over the head with condemnation of which self-condemnation is the worst. It makes us feel we have to have a period away from God to justify our punishment. After that period, then we deem us worthy to get back in His Presence.

Let's say that my parents were the king and queen of a land and I got lost. When I find my way again, I'm still the king and queen's child; my bloodline in the royal family remains. In reality, we're righteous through the bloodline of Jesus. If we mess up, we're still righteous. We're still holy. Leviticus 19:2 says, "You shall be holy, for I the Lord your God am holy." Holy means "to be set apart for God and His purpose." Our purpose never changes with God.

Sometimes we lose our way and step right up into God's holy

presence. We ask for His forgiveness and to be right with Him once again. Our right standing with God isn't based on what we do, but who Jesus is and what Jesus has already done.

LIFE LESSON: We may be foolish, turn away or get out of line, but our position with God is always secure.

MY PRAYER: Thank You, Jesus, that when I mess up, You are always there to raise me up and secure me in Your love. Your forgiveness is forever and Your love is never-ending. I can stand in Your holy presence and be secure in Your love.

HIS PROMISE:
"There is therefore now no condemnation for those who are in Christ Jesus."
— Romans 8:1

"But God, being rich in mercy, because of the great love with which he loved us, and raised us with Him and seated us with Him in the heavenly places in Christ Jesus." — Ephesians 2:4-6

ABOUT DIANA SCOTHORN

Diana R. Scothorn is an ordained Minister of the Gospel. She is Founder and owner of The Benefit Link Inc. incorporated in 2007 as a Market Place Ministry and licensed in all 50 States. She works together with her husband and CEO, Stewart D. Scothorn, also an ordained Minister.

Her corporation serves seniors that are in need of compassion and guidance when getting on Medicare and facing the challenge of the Medicare maize, as well as a season of change. Diana had been recognized 25 consecutive years as being Number One in her field across the United States. She has been featured in Society Magazine as Successful businesswomen of the Year 2018, 2019, 2020, 2021 and 2022.

Her heart is to influence the Market Place as a platform to point people to Jesus. Her and her husband have a heart to fund the Kingdom and advance the gospel. Diana has traveled 10 years abroad to help support missions in Europe and South America.

She is a public and International Speaker. A popular speaker at women's conferences, she was one of the key note speakers in Women Conference in Brazil, sponsored through Global Advance. She also spoke in South America, at a marketplace conference, with an emphasis on using your business platform as a Ministry.

She has a heart for women, and strives to help women have a strong spiritual, mental, and physical core. Her background has an emphasis on fitness, and health. She worked for Richard Simons, and supervised all ladies' health clubs for 10 years in the early years of her career.

She and her husband serve on the Board of Terri Savelle Ministries, and in the President's Cabinet with Jerry Savelle Ministry. You can connect with her on Instagram and Facebook. She has Daily Devotionals on Facebook as she encourages and inspires people to live in victory.